LESSONS FROM A CHURCH IN
ZOMBIE LAND

LESSONS FROM A CHURCH IN ZOMBIE LAND

Rob Bryceson

Street Wise
Spokane, WA

Publishing
733 West Garland Ave. Spokane, WA 99205
United States of America
51499

ISBN 13: 978-1-94777-850-4
ISBN 10: 1947778501
Library of Congress © 2017 Rob Bryceson.
All Rights Reserved.
No part of this book may be reproduced, scanned, or distributed in any printed or electronic form without permission.

First Edition: November 2017
Printed in the United States of America

Edited by Ted L. Carroll

Cover Art by Jeremy Wittington
Design by Danielle Mize

"Scripture taken from the NEW AMERICAN STANDARD BIBLE®, Copyright©1960,1962,1963,1968,1971,1972,1973,1975,1977,1995 by The Lockman Foundation. Used by permission."

THE HOLY BIBLE, NEW INTERNATIONAL VERSION®, NIV® Copyright © 1973, 1978, 1984, 2011 by Biblica, Inc.® Used by permission. All rights reserved worldwide.

To my beautiful, steadfast, incredible wife! It's impossible to explain how much you have endured on this journey. I dedicate this book to you my warrior princess. No matter how deep the fight or overwhelming the challenge, you picked up your sword and shield and entered the battle fearlessly. I love you.

CONTENTS

SECTION 1: PERSONAL APOCOLYPTIC FALLOUT

1. YOU GOTTA DO SOMETHING ABOUT RED ROB .... Page 2
2. I THINK THE EMPEROR MIGHT BE NAKED .... Page 5
3. MARCHING OUT OF STEP .... Page 7
4. MY OWN PERSONAL NINEVEH .... Page 11
5. KNOCK, KNOCK, KNOCKING ON HEAVEN'S DOOR .... Page 15

SECTION 2: A ZOMBIE CHURCH

6. A ZOMBIE CHURCH .... Page 22
7. CHILI AND CORNBREAD .... Page 27
8. CHURCH RULES .... Page 32
9. PREACHING GOOD NEWS TO THE ZOMBIFIED .... Page 36
10. GOD HUNTS US DOWN FOR ANOTHER CHANCE .... Page 39
11. WHAT WOULD YOU SAY? .... Page 41

SECTION 3: SURVIVAL IN ZOMBIELAND

12. I GUESS I'M CRAZY .... Page 46
13. LOOKING UP AT THE UNDERBELLY OF THE AMERICAN CHURCH Page 48
14. BITING THE WRONG HAND .... Page 50
15. THE ACTUAL MISSION .... Page 55
16. TIMING IS EVERYTHING .... Page 58

SECTION 4: LIFE AMONG THE WALKING DEAD

17. LIVING IN A PARALLEL UNIVERSE .... Page 66
18. PLACEBO CHRISTIANITY & A CLASH OF TEEN CULTURE Page 69
19. JUST MAYBE .... Page 72
20. THE POWER OF SMALL THINGS .... Page 76
21. THE NATURE OF PREACHING .... Page 80
22. ETHICAL DILEMMAS .... Page 82
23. FOR EMERGENCY, TRY SERVICE .... Page 85
24. A TRAILER LOAD OF GRACE .... Page 88
25. SCATTERING SEED .... Page 91

26. JUST WHEN I'D HAD ENOUGH .... Page 94
27. I WOULDN'T HAVE THOUGHT OF THAT .... Page 99
28. GOD WATCHING .... Page 102

SECTION 5: THE SAFETY ZONE IS COMPROMISED

29. I LIKES TO SITS IN CHURCH .... Page 108
30. TO SAVE A LIFE - OR NOT?! .... Page 112
31. THIRD WORLD CHURCH IN A FIRST WORLD NATION .. Page 116
32. STRANGERS AND ANGELS .... Page 119
33. YA JUST NEVER KNOW .... Page 121
34. TOILET PAPER AND HOPE .... Page 125
35. BLOG COMMENTS AND A JAR OF COINS .... Page 129
36. CAN ANYONE HELP? .... Page 131

SECTION 6: DYING AMONG THE INFECTED

37. CHANGE - IT'S THE ONLY CONSTANT .... Page 138
38. LEATHER COUCHES .... Page 142
39. WHEELING AND DEALING .... Page 147
40. PARACHUTING IN .... Page 151
41. DING DONG .... Page 156
42. 125 . . . AND COUNTING .... Page 160

SECTION 7: THE FINAL ESCAPE PLAN

43. COFFEE IN TWENTY YEARS .... Page 168
44. RUMBLINGS ON SEATTLE FAULT LINES .... Page 172
45. DYING ON THE TABLE .... Page 178
46. CHURCH IS A DIRTY WORD .... Page 185
47. BREATHING .... Page 190
48. I CAN'T TALK ABOUT IT .... Page 197
49. ANGEL AND THE PROPHET .... Page 202

ABOUT THE AUTHOR .... Page 208

WE HAVE ALL BEEN THE WALKING DEAD, THOSE WHO HAVE COME ALIVE ARE STILL CALLED TO LIVE AMONG THEM.

As for you, you were dead in your transgressions and sins, in which you used to live when you followed the ways of this world and of the ruler of the kingdom of the air, the spirit who is now at work in those who are disobedient. All of us also lived among them at one time, gratifying the cravings of our flesh and following its desires and thoughts. Like the rest, we were by nature deserving of wrath. But because of his great love for us, God, who is rich in mercy, made us alive with Christ even when we were dead in transgressions—it is by grace you have been saved.

Ephesians 2:1-5 New American Standard Bible (NASB)

SECTION 1: PERSONAL APOCOLYPTIC FALLOUT

But we have this treasure in earthen vessels, so that the surpassing greatness of the power will be of God and not from ourselves; we are afflicted in every way, but not crushed; perplexed, but not despairing; persecuted, but not forsaken; struck down, but not destroyed; always carrying about in the body the dying of Jesus, so that the life of Jesus also may be manifested in our body. For we who live are constantly being delivered over to death for Jesus' sake, so that the life of Jesus also may be manifested in our mortal flesh. So death works in us, but life in you.

2 Corinthians 4:7-12 (NASB)

1. YOU GOTTA DO SOMETHING ABOUT RED ROB

Our little inner-city church of eighty people was feeding an average of 150 homeless and poor people on Sunday afternoons year-round. One day, during one of the meals, a guy came up to me very upset.

"You gotta do something about Red Rob. You *gotta* do something about him!" he growled in an angry, aggressive tone.

"Calm down" I said, "I'm not sure I even know what you're talking about. What's going on?"

"You know that alleyway you have behind the church?"

I knew what he was talking about. The office entrance was on the back side of the building sandwiched between the building and the alley. It was about six feet wide and twenty feet long. An eight-foot-tall retaining wall on the alley side created a really nice, rarely used, slightly hidden area to hide out, catch a nap, camp, or pee. My office window was right there looking out into that little alley.

"Well me and my lady been camping back there at night," he confided, adding hurriedly, "We keep it real nice and clean and sweep up after ourselves, just so you know" as if to ease any concerns I might have about them sleeping on church property. "Well, the other night me and the old lady was gettin' it on. And I looked up, and there was Red Rob sitting on the steps smoking a cigarette watching us! You gotta do something about him!" he finished shouting in rage.

I thought to myself, "You're having outdoor, public sex on church property right outside my office window and you want me to do something about the guy sitting on the steps smoking cigarettes watching you?"

Now, I have a master's in divinity degree from seminary and had to take advanced pastoral counseling courses at the graduate level to get that degree. I know you're not going to believe this, but in all that training and graduate level prepare-them-for-church-ministry work, somehow . . . . . this one never came up.

I mumbled something about how things would change in less than two weeks when we planned on tearing out all the juniper bushes on that side of the building, one of which Red Rob used as his place of residence, then they would all have to move on and no one would be living on the property at night. So, problem solved.

Red Rob came up to me a while later, slightly wobbly and definitely drunk, which was the only state I'd ever seen him in. "I gotsha con-fesh-shun to make" he drawled out in a slurry manner, hanging his head in shame. "I'ze busted dah winda on th'uther shide of the build'n," he sloppily sighed with a heavy shrug of his shoulders while his arms hung limply at his sides.

We had five very tall windows in our 1950 sanctuary building along the main drag of Division Street on the east side of the property. The bottom panels of four of them had been broken and replaced with plywood. The fifth bottom panel turned up broken when we arrived at church that day.

"So, you broke the window?" I asked doubtfully, since he was a very harmless guy and I had already heard the story earlier from another of our patrons who eats at our meals and also attends church. "Well I heard that you and Geoff got into a fight over something" (now I knew what it was), "And that he shoved your head into the window and that's how it broke."

"Well I ain't one ta snitcsh ya know, but thatsh true," He admitted. "But it was *my* head dat broke it so I'ze pay for it when I can."

I wasn't planning on waiting for him to send in a check any time soon.

I walked away from that conversation, and many others like it, wondering how I got into this place. What possible skills and talents did I have to pastor such rough crowds in such a crazy environment? What was God thinking putting me here? Every week I met with the walking dead who shuffled through life bent with pain, rejection, addiction, abuse, and violence. It was ministry among the zombies of America.

I admit I was learning a lot. I was being challenged to rethink some ideas and rediscover the love God has for the lost and broken in our society. I was learning to join him in loving the "least of these" (Matthew 25:40) and it wasn't easy.

It would take me several years and numerous mistakes to finally learn what I needed to know and unlearn much of what I had been taught in my previous years of ministry to work effectively among the poor in a downtown urban church. I still don't know half of what I should know and in all honesty, I'm probably not very good at it, even after all this time.

We are hearing so much in recent years about people who want to get active working in social justice causes and how the average church attendee wants to roll up their sleeves and get dirty helping the poor. They aren't satisfied as passive listeners anymore. Recent best sellers in the Christian book industry by authors like Francis Chan, David Pratt, Donald Miller and others have tapped into an underlying angst and given voice to the restless frustrations of a seemingly dormant Evangelical Christian community when it comes to social justice and compassion ministry. We are told by online Christian celebrity bloggers how the church is inadequate to reach the millennial generation because we don't understand their passion to be directly involved in such works.

But after several years of doing downtown urban ministry, I will say that in general the American Church is woefully ill-prepared, poorly equipped, and under-trained to be very effective. Many of our Bible colleges and seminaries lack the experience to teach and train the next generation to be prepared for all they will encounter if they even try to step out and work among the poor.

We don't champion the right leaders in our church world in order to learn from the best. We don't honor the skill and learning of the social worker in our colleges, on church staffs, or at our seminars and workshops. At our retreats, conferences, seminars, or denominational meetings we rarely ever give the microphone to a small urban church pastor who knows poverty culture.

We have been way too enamored by church growth experts and we have been mesmerized by celebrity, suburban leaders who have huge church followings. Those are the voices to which we have been listening when discussing church ministry. We have little idea how much we don't know and how unprepared we are with our stock ministry answers, answers that can often sound like Pinterest postcard sentiments. When it comes to tackling social justice and poverty issues our church growth principles come across like a suit and tie on the farm. And in the Evangelical community – we don't play well with others and always try to start and do things by ourselves.

The following stories will give you a small glimpse into the world of the urban poverty church. You will get glimpses of who the walking dead are in our society. Those who have had nothing but Apocalypse in their personal histories.

You may discover how it differs from many of our preconceived notions about how to pastor and lead effectively. If you step off the beaten paths of church work and wander into the jungle of poverty culture, you will soon realize much of what you know is useless. Many of the areas where you are firmly grounded will be shaken. You'd better have a sharp machete of wisdom because many of your patterned church responses and answers won't cut through the pain, trauma, and outlandishness of poverty. You also better get used to being dirty. But, you will have a great adventure!

2. I THINK THE EMPEROR MIGHT BE NAKED

I once had a about a dynamic relationship with Jesus through a deeply committed community of friends and loved ones in the kind of church I wanted to attend and the kind of ministry I wanted to do. I dreamed about the community that I wistfully imagined serving. I desired the intimate relationships I would build in a church setting that was both artistic and intellectually stimulating. I longed for a compassion-driven organization that was oriented toward social justice, authenticity, and love. I tried to plant just such a ministry once, but it failed, and after four years, four months, and four days – it closed.

I had given my life to Jesus after watching a friend drown on my very first youth group trip at the age of fifteen. I suppose I ran pretty hot and cold for most of life since then. Sometimes my faith and life were strong and at other times, I tried to turn my back and walk away – but couldn't. Eventually I would work my way up the ladder of Christian ministry, first through music and worship, and then into teaching and preaching.

I held key lay leadership positions from youth worker to worship leader at several churches. I would earn a graduate Certificate in Ministry as well as a Masters in Divinity from seminary. By the time I turned forty, I had pretty much seen it all. I've been on paid staff at six different churches and served at another four as a lay leader or unpaid worship leader. I've served in seven different denominations, from Pentecostal to Presbyterian and I have been on staff in small, medium, and mega churches. I've been a recording artist, worship song writer, program director, small group pastor, adult education director, teaching pastor, church planter, and senior pastor. I have sung, counseled, taught, and traveled up and down the west coast. I've attended numerous conferences, training workshops, and advanced seminars. I've read hundreds of books on church, on ministry, and about God.

But, in the summer of 2008, I was pretty much disillusioned and frustrated with my Christian experience. I was so exasperated by church that I was ready to walk away from it all to go do something else with my skills and talents. I don't mean walk away from Jesus or his words. I mean *church*. I mean the institution we have built in America; the programmatic, market driven, consumer focused, production event, which we call church. So, I tried to leave it all.

It's kind of ironic, but it was also four years, four months and four days after the final service of my church plant that a moving truck, like some great fish, took us to the state of Washington, vomiting my family and me up on the shores of my hometown; a town I left twenty years earlier vowing never, ever to return - my own personal Nineveh.

This is the story of how I came to minister against my will and desires in a downtown, urban setting of Americana. It is a reflection of all my previous years of training and experience in church and ministry, sifted through the iron grate of poverty and brokenness encountered in the deep pits of a population which was enduring homelessness, addiction, mental illness, and suffering. It is my story, along with a collection of my insights and observations, which I have gathered from being so far outside of the box that the view is no longer uniform or geometric – in short, not even box shaped. I hope that this story inspires you and challenges you to reflect on your own ideas and experiences and hopefully, you will see Jesus and yourself differently.

It's common in many Christian books for the author to do a lot of the thinking for the reader. You will find that I trust my readers won't mind it if I don't always resolve the delicate or difficult ethical dilemmas with a nice little Band-Aid Bible verse or pithy little serendipitous quote. I think you are probably smart enough and deep enough in your own faith journey that if you have picked up this book and are reading this, then you are somewhat disillusioned yourself. Maybe you feel as I have felt when gazing at American church that, "The Emperor Has No Clothes". But you feel like you'd better not say anything because everyone else is cheering so strongly while you think, the reality is it's rather naked, skinny and unimpressive. Perhaps you are looking for deeper answers to faith and life. My guess is that you too, have wondered why the American church is so powerful and rich on the one hand, and so socially insignificant on the other hand.

We no longer shape culture; we react to it – usually against it. In my time pastoring in the trenches and gutters at the bottom of society looking up – I have found new views of the underbelly of American Christianity. It isn't always a pretty a view but sometimes on certain occasions, at the right angles, it can be inspiring!

Eventually we all come full circle, realizing that the institution of church was often naked. The Emperor isn't though. He sits on his throne still doing the real work by the power of his spirit, often in unexpected places with unexpected people.

3. MARCHING OUT OF STEP

When the church I planted closed, my dream died. I know a piece of me died too. I still can't quite describe what was lost, but

I know I'm not the same guy. I don't have the same confidence, the same drive, the same direction, the same hunger for God. My pace is slower, my observations greater and to be honest, my expectations are lower.

As the church plant was shutting down, I sat with a group of pastor friends from other area churches baring my soul. I was hurt, dazed and confused. This group of guys had been meeting with each other for a couple of years just to share thoughts ideas, personal and church issues in a safe setting.

"What do you think you will do now?" one of them asked me in a concerned manner.

"I don't know. Sometimes I think I just want to maybe go lead worship in a church somewhere for a year or so and dry out."

I had no direction, no goals, no specific dreams for my life in ministry anymore. Playing guitar and leading worship was really a fallback skill I had because I'd been doing it for so long and I'm good at it.

A week later the local Presbyterian pastor, who was part of that group, asked me for coffee and said, "I want to offer you that job."

"What job"?

"The one where you lead worship for a year and dry out" he grinned slyly.

Their church had recently been through a split when the associate pastor had tried to lead a coup against him. Their bylaws required a vote to dismiss an ordained pastor and months had been spent maneuvering with political intrigue and clandestine meetings on the part of the associate against the pastor and the board. When the congregation finally voted it was 124 approving the dismissal of the associate and 115 against. He was fired, angry words were flung at the pastor and the board by his followers, and a good portion of the people left. That had been only eight months earlier. The church wasn't even close to having recovered. It wasn't going to be an easy job to take—and they were Presbyterian. They were a choir robe wearing, hymnbook singing, pipe organ playing group. They wanted to learn to *get contemporary*. I'm an old-grown bluesy, rock-n-roller. I thought I belonged there as much as a milk bucket under a bull.

In the months preceding laying down my church plant, I kept having people tell me that God wasn't finished with me yet. They told me how he had bigger and greater things in store for me. They prophesied that I was not yet even in my promised land, let alone ready to settle down and occupy territory. Helping liturgical Presbyterians learn to clap at all, let alone on beats two and four, wasn't what I had in mind for a move up.

I thought the only way I would be sent to a wounded, liturgical, traditional, Presbyterian Church was as penance for my sins. It turns out I'm a bigger sinner than I thought because I signed a one-year contract to help them out and spent the next four years there.

It was tough going at first, because I only play guitar not piano and some of them simply didn't appreciate the instrument. Others didn't like the contemporary style. They show emotion and move like, well, like Scottish Presbyterians. One guy on the worship team told me I was the "Abomination That Causes Desolation in the Sanctuary". He surprisingly quit the worship team. But, I would make some outstanding friends there – many whom I cherish today. I had some great times and added about sixty hymns to my repertoire, a bunch of which I still play today.

We did a blended single service for the first year, giving the congregation a chance to combine their remaining strength in one room at one time and so they began healing. At the end of the first year the leadership came to me asking me for a longer commitment. They had bought some land several years previously and they were getting an offer on the current building for 5 million. They wanted to take that, combine it with another 5 million they planned on borrowing and then move to the new location. The actual construction and move would take 2-3 more years. My two oldest daughters were freshmen in high school. I agreed to stay through the process until they graduated.

It was kind of obvious from God anyway because at the end of that year I still wasn't sure about my own healing and the drying out process wasn't anywhere near complete. We divided into two services that next season, one traditional and one contemporary and took off flying.

As the architectural plans and ideas unfolded, I knew I didn't belong. Every time I contributed an idea or expressed opinions about the worship setup and tech issues, I was vetoed or shot down. They changed the church name in the process to something innocuous, trendy, corporate, and vague. I didn't care for the design, wasn't inspired by the ideas, and realized right away that they were building their own dream house. It wasn't one I wanted to live in, but I would do my best to help them create it and then move on.

A total of ten million bucks of God's money got spent on that project. It was nice, but not my style. What bothered me most was that when the move finally happened no new ministries were created or launched. All the things we did at the old site were exactly what we did at the new site. We had a paid preschool before and we had one now, although the new one was better designed. Nothing new was done in youth ministry, the children's ministry had a bigger field for games, but the new preschool dominated what they could do in classrooms. They built the exact same platform layout they already had. They were virtually the same seating capacity. They did the same services only now, there were no rooms for adult Sunday classes or counseling. Nothing was created for social justice or compassion ministries.

I thought some new ministry should be created, some new identity established, some new opportunity to change society should be instituted. I thought there should be something tangible in the ministry arena that warranted the spending an extra five million dollars of God's money beyond what they had already to do something new which couldn't be done before. If all that was accomplished meant having a more visible location by which to market ourselves, then it seemed like a grand waste to me.

Everyone else seemed to be enjoying the ride though. They all seemed to be marching in uniformed step with enthusiasm and no questioning. I knew my stride and gate wasn't matching. I was as comfortable as a redneck in a coat and tie trying to blend in at a society party. I smiled a lot and helped where I could, mostly staying out of the way. The best help I provided was through my previous experiences doing portable church. I helped them organize, plan and engineer for ease and practicality during the one year they went portable between selling the old place and moving into the new one.

I got their permission to begin looking toward my own future and started applying for work. I sent resumes from Main to Australia – literally. No one wanted me. I got one interview in that year and the church chose the other guy. I wasn't good enough to be seriously considered. Churches want tested and proven champions in leadership and church growth. I'm certainly not a champion or hero.

4. MY OWN PERSONAL NINEVEH

I thought that since I wasn't a fit where I was and some of my best spiritual gifts were being wasted, it was time to move along and find my future, which I hoped would be some blissful ministry with Jesus somewhere exotic. I was counting on the affirmations that all those people had been telling me saying, "God has something better for you!" couldn't be wrong. But they were.

We knew early on that 2008 would be a big year for us. The current church would move into its new facility that year. Our two oldest, the twins, were going to graduate high school. The two younger daughters would be entering their freshman and sophomore years that coming September and our son was going to enter sixth grade. Sixth grade is the beginning of middle school in California. In 2007, we knew we had one year before all that change would go down and then the window of opportunity to make a big location change would close. The summer of 2008 was crucial to make something happen. We had little more than a year for God to reveal to us his perfect will and plan.

In the early part of 2007, I was sending out resumes to find God's perfect fit for me when the housing market crashed like a wet cardboard box full of your favorite china. Our house lost over $250,000 of value, which it probably never really had thanks to the shysters in the banking and appraisal industry. I still had no offers for work and could see the writing on the wall. My family was in financial freefall with no parachute.

By the time the twins were graduating, it was apparent that we couldn't stay in our home and there was nowhere to go. I had no offers, no interviews, and no opportunities. We began talking about what we would do. The schools were in crisis, the job market in the hole, the home we lived in for 17 years but only managed to buy three years before, was going to be lost.

We discussed what was most important in life and decided that church had eaten up so much of our life and years, always coming first, always driving our most important decisions, that we were sick of investing in it. We just didn't want to drag the family behind that horse anymore. I had looked and searched for some other opportunity only to discover that the career path I had followed, ministry – didn't want me.

We asked ourselves - What if we put the kids totally first? What if we picked a lifestyle in a place they wanted? For our son that meant the rugged outdoors. What if we picked somewhere to live where the schools were better? How about where they had extended family? We had lived so far from other relatives for all their lives because of church ministry that they didn't really know their cousins, aunts, uncles or grandparents all that well.

In the summer of 2008 we quit the job, short sold our home, and moved lock-stock-and-barrel back to Spokane Washington. At the time, we had no jobs to go to, nowhere to live, and no known future. Our plan was to put our stuff in storage, stay with relatives or in a hotel, let the kids pick the school they wanted to attend, then find a place to rent in that district while looking for jobs to support us. We were going to simply crash-land and start over in life. We had about three months of savings. We just knew we wanted out of ministry. It had not produced a good life for us after investing so much.

I was not anxious to go to Spokane. It wasn't a great place for me what with it holding bad memories from my first twenty-five-plus years of growing up there. I had left twenty years before, vowing to never go back, but the extended family wanted us so much they paid for a moving truck to get us there.

One of my old friends owned several rental homes days before moving he called saying one just became vacant and we could stay there with our stuff paying whatever we could for rent until we got settled. It was in a neighborhood full of the kind of people who would guest star on Jerry Springer, but the deal was good. It was just the kind of brief rescue we needed.

Upon arrival, my mom, who now lived in Arizona most of the year, ended up selling a building in downtown Spokane she hadn't planned to sell, but the offer was too good to turn down. She reinvested the capital gains in a house of our choosing located in a school district the kids picked. We only needed jobs to complete our transition. I thought my wife had a better chance than I to get a job with her administrative, corporate skill set. That would turn out to be wrong.

We settled into the rental, got the kids registered in the school of their choice and began looking for work. At the same time, we were looking for a house to reinvest the capital gains my mom had. I was more than nervous being asked what payments I could afford when neither my wife nor I had a job! I don't recommend this strategy as a life plan.

Spokane was always a cursed job market for me. That's one of the reasons I left, vowing to never go back. It held too many memories of living in poverty, scraping by to make a living. We hit Craigslist and the newspaper every day while trying to tap every friendship or connection I ever had to find a job, so we could restart our lives.

Tonia, my wife, has a skill set in hospitality, administration, and organization. She was applying for twenty, or so, positions a day and getting almost nowhere. We couldn't even get a return call or an email response saying, "Thank you, for your application." It was frustrating. Out of twenty jobs listed only three or four mentioned specifically the name of the company and where to apply.

One afternoon Tonia went downtown to a cute, little, boutique hotel that had an open front desk position. We went together, and I waited at the back of the lobby while she walked up to the main desk to hand in a resume and fill out an application. When she finished, she just handed the pieces of paper back across the counter to this pretty girl (who had all the personality of oatmeal). Tonia then turned and walked out. I caught her at the door.

"What are you doing? You know better than that. You aren't strong on paper and you're *way* better in person. Have her call the manager down, hand your application to him and chit chat for a moment or two. You know you're *not* strong on paper buy you *are* in person! That girl is going to file your resume under a pile of papers which the manger will never see, or she'll simply trash it. Come on baby, you know better than that!"

"No, I don't think so. I can feel the energy here it's really bad and I don't think I want the job anyway." She retorted. Tonia has a very strong spiritual gift of discernment and she's always right. The place would turn out to sell to another hotel thirty days later and they would lay off the entire staff to restart. But at the time, we didn't know that.

"Look honey, we can't be choosy right now." I pressed her, "One of us needs a job fast. We're out of savings in about a month and we need to get some income, or we will be in a world of hurt. Take the job and if it stinks keep looking until you find something better."

She then started giving me grief about how she was doing all the work to find a job and I was doing nothing. Of course, I informed her how wrong she was. I only knew church work for the last twenty plus years and getting a job in ministry was different.

"If you want me to get a job doing what I've always done then I needed to network people and meet pastors and discover who has positions open and what kind of churches they are and so forth and so on. It's all done by personal networking in the ministry world", I explained in an exasperated fashion.

"A guy doesn't just lookup *pastor* on craigslist. You don't find ministry jobs by reading the newspaper want ads," I admonished.

Even after my intelligent explanations, she still wouldn't listen to me; *can you imagine?*

So, I told her I would dig a resume out of my briefcase in the backseat and drop it off at the first church we saw.

5. KNOCK, KNOCK, KNOCKING ON HEAVEN'S DOOR

We were downtown Spokane and I drove about ten blocks or so stopping at an old, worn-down looking, brick church. I knew it was there. Everyone knew it was there. It sat a block off the interstate and kitty-corner from a landmark burger joint on the main drag (which spans the entire city, north and south). Literally fifty-thousand cars a day drive by this church. Everyone living in the area has driven past it hundreds of times. It's been sitting there since I was a kid – even longer. In truth, it's been sitting on that corner since 1905.

I can drive an hour any compass direction and mention the big brick church kitty-corner from Dick's Burgers downtown and they say, "The one they tore down a few years back?"

"No, the other one that's still standing," I reply.

"Oh. I really liked the one they tore down. That was a nice building."

I've had that conversations fifty times. All the way deep into the Idaho panhandle and once while riding four-wheelers way up in the backwoods up along the Canadian border two hour's drive north. I've had that conversation a couple hour's drive south while hunting pheasant in the rolling wheat fields of the Palouse. Everyone knows the church I'm talking about. But I've only met *one* person who ever knew the name of the church. *I* didn't know the name of the church and I've probably passed it over a thousand times in my life.

I pulled into the parking lot situated in the roughest part of downtown, got out of the car and went to the first door I saw. It was locked. So was the next one, and the next, and the next. I went all the way around the building knocking on all six doors. I noticed the name, First Covenant, on the far side when I rounded the corner after doorway number four.

I was confused by that because I had been part of the Evangelical Covenant Denomination when I planted a church in 2000. Usually the name Covenant is associated with us, but not always.

I had met the superintendent of the Pacific Northwest Region for the denomination in Denver several years before and asked him if there were any Covenant churches in Spokane. I was interested to know if the denomination I was now a part of in California had any sister churches in my home town. But being a superintendent, he was used to pastors asking him about job opportunities so he understood my question to be whether or not there was a pastoral position available in Spokane.

He informed me, "No we don't have anything in Spokane," meaning, "No jobs available."

I misunderstood thinking he meant we have no Covenant churches in Spokane, so I had spent the last several years believing that there was no connection with my denomination in my home town. When I saw the church name for the first time, I thought it might be a coincidence or a different "covenant."

At the sixth and final door, down a little alleyway with broken glass (which smelled like pee) I saw a buzzer and hit it. I stood for a bit and there was no answer. As I was walking away, a silver-haired guy answered the door, "Can I help you?"

Since I was confused by the name I opened with, "Is this an Evangelical Covenant Church"?

"Yes" he said.

"You are part of the Evangelical Covenant Church, headquartered in Chicago?" I asked, dumbfounded; then continued, "But I was informed there were no Covenant churches in Spokane," I stammered.

"That's because we're seen as an embarrassment and they don't want to admit we're here," he replied.

"How long have you been here?"

"One hundred and twenty years," he matter-of-factly informed me.

"Well, I should think they might have heard about you by now," I thought to myself.

We talked for several minutes. He had been there for eighteen years. He invited me into a little cubby of a reception area with war-weary, stained carpet and two to three desks too many packed into the confined space. It had stacks of paper and old Yellow Page phone books piled high everywhere you looked. There was a ratty old couch that Goodwill would throw away, if one tried to donate it. The paint was dingy white. The one wallpapered wall was peeling in several spots.

He gave me a grand tour of the place. It was old, dirty, run-down, dark, depressing, un-kept, untouched, unrepaired, and unloved. The people calling the shots must have been hoarders because every little room of the poorly designed space was packed with old junk. No one wanted to be responsible for throwing something away that might turn out to be needed later. Every piece of ugly worn out furniture that folks got sick of at home they brought down to donate to the church. The paint looked original, in both the 1950 building and the 1929 children's wing. The computer at the desk looked like it might have been brand new the same year the operating system came out. It was running *Windows 95*.

After the tour, I told him I was new in town and looking for a ministry position. I thought he would know someone hiring or know of something I could apply for, since he'd been pastoring in the area for almost twenty years. I handed him a left-over resume from my year and half of looking for work.

"Oh, we're looking for a worship leader," He said excitedly.

Fat chance, I thought. I had seen the pipe organ and choir loft. "Oh, well good luck on your search," I replied in a hopeful tone. "But if you know of some *other* job, feel free to pass my name along." And I parted company. I returned to a smiling wife still sitting in the car a half our later.

"Well?" she asked with a smirk on her face.

"They have a job opening," I replied in the most disgusted tone I could muster.

She laughed.

Meanwhile, all the other job opportunities I was exploring fell through. All the other connections failed to materialize into anything at all. I applied for some ministry jobs out of desperation, but I think I scared and intimidated a couple of other pastors with my experiences and other churches found themselves cutting back in the tough economy and not replacing their positions.

The First Covenant pastor and I had coffee. It turned out they were almost out of business. He was buying the parsonage and generating a hefty amount of cash for the church to throw at a staff position for worship and outreach to help them revitalize and give them one more chance at a future. They were down to about thirty people. He had performed seventy funerals in his time there. I was amazed that he had a congregation twice the size under the ground as above it. Their last bit of savings was running out.

Against my better judgment, personal ambitions, and emotional desires, I spoke and led worship the following Sunday as a candidate. The pastor did announcements. They voted thirty-eight to one to hire me. Obviously, extra people came out that Sunday to see what I was all about. I started working there two weeks later.

We were in a rough part of town with a homeless men's shelter a block away and a homeless women's shelter a block in the other direction. Spokane Mental Health was half a block down the street, prison work release apartments were behind us in the alley, a men's drug rehab shelter was located across the parking lot, and numerous little dirty slumlord apartments surrounded us. The area also boasted several run-down transient hotels where convicts stayed when they were released back to society. Addicts, drunkards, and prostitutes completely surrounded us.

We got a regular flow of transients into the church. My second Sunday there, one came through to meet with the pastor to explain that he couldn't get his stuff out of the Howard Johnson across the street, because Greyhound had bought the room for him and his name wasn't on the receipt. He was a little drunk and said he needed prayer.

The pastor began to pray, but was interrupted when the transient raised his arms to heaven and in a loud and slurred voice cried out "Oh, Lord, I've been watching this church from across the street all day. Help them do what they're trying to do. Give them help Lord to become what they're supposed to become. Help them see what you want them to see and do what you want them to do." He sloshed to a close as his arms came down swinging at his sides.

Listen my friend —when a drunken, homeless, vagabond prays that God help YOU then you know you're in a pretty bad way.

This was my welcome to my upwardly mobile career. I kept hearing, "God has a plan," though, so that should count for something. I knew we had about one year to turn things around. But then again, my last one-year gig lasted four years. Little did I know or expect that this one-year gig would find me in that building, holding down a pastoral job for six more years.

SECTION 2: A ZOMBIE CHURCH

For those who are according to the flesh set their minds on the things of the flesh, but those who are according to the Spirit, the things of the Spirit. For the mind set on the flesh is death, but the mind set on the Spirit is life and peace, because the mind set on the flesh is hostile toward God; for it does not subject itself to the law of God, for it is not even able to do so, because the mind set on the flesh is hostile toward God; for it does not subject itself to the law of God, for it is not even able *to do so.*

Romans 8:5-7 (NASB)

6. A ZOMBIE CHURCH

On Sunday, November 2nd, 2008, we drove to our first day on the job at First Covenant Church in Spokane, Washington. I was officially on staff and committed to seeing to its health and vitality.

On the way to church it dawned on my family and me that we hadn't really attended a service there yet. The only time we had been there, I led all the worship and preached the sermon. With more than a little anxiety, my wife and I wondered what we were in for. I was slated that day to only sing three songs and then I would sit back and see what else happened.

That morning we would sit through an hour and forty-two minutes of what I consider (to this day) the worst church service I have ever attended in my entire life. Before things began, no one greeted us or said hello. I entered with my wife and three of our five kids. The other two were off at college. We were hard to miss. We sat among thirty or so people scattered in little pockets among the twelve-foot-long double rows of solid oak pews.

People seemed to purposefully avoid looking at us, which felt awkward, like one does with that homeless guy who is flying a cardboard sign on the street corner right beside your car. The rest of the congregation were scattered in little groups about the room which sat around two hundred. I found out later that this was because they didn't like each other much.

The service started with a dirge on the pipe organ for the prelude. I don't know what the hymn was, but it obviously communicated a tone that said, "Come and act proper, pay your respects, someone has died." The mood in the room matched it.

The second thing in the order of service was for the congregation to stand and sing an old classic out of the hymnbook accompanied by pipe organ. Even though I'm an old rocker, my years at the Presbyterian Church under the fantastic organist they had taught me to appreciate the powerful instrument. When played well, it's inspiring. This hymn wasn't inspiring. It was sickly and spindly, like a malnourished third-world child one sees in a missionary brochure. The next thing to go down was the announcements, which had all the satiating power of drinking dust. Immediately following that was the greeting time.

The pastor looked out over the vastly empty space and said, "Is there anyone here who has a brought a friend and you would like to introduce? . . . . anyone? . . . . anyone? . . . . Perhaps you're new here visiting with us and you would like to introduce yourself? . . . . anyone? . . . . anyone? . . . . . Well then," turning to me he added, "Let's continue in worship."

I got up to play my three songs, with that inspiring hand-off. The service just went downhill after that. When I asked why they did that "visitor introduction" in the greeting time, I was informed it was to reinforce to the congregation that they aren't inviting people and that's why they aren't growing.

"I'm pretty sure they already know they aren't inviting their friends. And they know why too," I quipped.

"Well, you've been brought on board to help us revitalize. What do you think?" the pastor asked me the next day.

"I have good news and bad news," I responded. "The good news is I think I know why people aren't coming. The bad news is – all of you – must be willing to change EVERYTHING you do here. Are you willing?"

"Oh, yes," was the answer he and others would give me. But they lied, of course. They were living in the carcass of a dead church past, with no life in them at all. It was a zombie church. It just kept going though, walking, but as a dead.

Any change was a fight, anything new was forbidden. Whole regions of the church fell under this person's or that person's territorial domain, and even though those ministries were long since dead there was no attempt to change a thing.

One room was full of thousands of copies of choir music. But they hadn't had a choir in over fifteen years. Another was full of fabric and buttons and thread but the women's sewing ministry died in a bitter grudge a decade before. Every idea they had to help the church was always a plan to revive some ministry that had long since died before because it was ineffective or outdated. But try to alter things or bring in something new and there was hell to pay with someone. The people were cowering in fear of the wrath of some parishioner, who had started such and such a ministry many years before. Sometimes they kept activities that were launched and run by people who were still considered members even though they had left the church years ago.

I learned people were considered members of the church if they were related by blood, marriage, Swedish ethnicity, or a past track record of attendance, even if they hadn't set foot in the door for a decade. One girl was still listed as a member, but she had run off eight years earlier, moved to Utah and married a Mormon, joining his church. But she was "so-and-so's daughter," so she was listed as an active member.

No ministry was ever critiqued or evaluated for its effectiveness. No goals or objectives were ever measured for staff, a ministry, or an activity. If an activity happened in the past it was considered valid regardless of attendance or participation. My wife tried to upgrade the children's ministry by instituting a children's check-in program for the nursery. We thought this was an especially good idea since there were forty-five registered sex offenders within eight blocks of the church. But, to our surprise, that was a battle too.

The small handful of people who had children treated the church like it was grandma's house and let their children run throughout the twelve thousand square-foot place at their pleasure. Asking them to monitor their children during church hours, or use a check-in and check-out procedure, was offensive to them. I can't tell you the number of times we found unattended little children playing in one of the many rooms upstairs in the church building, all alone. Changing that mindset proved impossible, despite the quality of the neighborhood.

We tried to rally the congregation together to hold meetings about revitalizing the church. We went through the list of active members to contact them by phone or email to discover who still wanted to be involved and who might be committed to help us rebuild. My wife accidently called the woman who was listed as head of the prayer chain and was promptly informed in the most disgusted manner that said leader had left the church 15 years earlier and had been faithfully attending a Presbyterian church a few miles away. Several of the members on the active membership list were literally dead already in the grave and had been for quite some time.

The church wasn't just demoralized; they were dysfunctional and broken – spiritually, socially, and psychologically. In a matter of weeks, my wife and I heard stories from different people about hurts, wounds, and bitterness that went back years. No grudge seemed too small not to be remembered and shared with newcomers. Bitterness, anger, and relational cowardice were the operating principles in the social construct.

I dug through the old archives and records to try and discover what went wrong. I discovered the church had been discussing closing since 1972. Any church that goes forty years discussing closing down every so often is not a dying church – it's a zombie church. They died already and just wouldn't stay down. Every few years, some member would pass on and leave an endowment that brought extended life. It worked like a mad scientist in Frankenstein's lab reanimating dead flesh, but it kept the beast going. *It's ALIIIIVE!* – but, not really.

That first year I felt like Eddie Albert's character, *Oliver* in the old TV show, *Green Acres*. It was a 1960s show about a New York lawyer and his high maintenance, glamorous wife (played by Eva Gabor) who moved to the rural hick town of Hooterville to take up his dream-life of farming. The premise of the show was that the whole town was kind of crazy and the antics revolved around the Eddie Albert character trying to explain reality to these hicks. Everything his wife and the town's folk did and the way they chose to do it was wacky but when he tried to correct them he was totally discombobulated by their illogical reasoning, which they portrayed as perfectly normal. Half the time, he ended up thinking he was the crazy one. I felt like Oliver that first year.

I could spend a long time telling stories of events that went down that year, some humorous, many shocking, several enraging, most absurd, but it wouldn't help much. I was slated to help them with outreach and growth, but I was having a difficult time convincing them they needed to change their environment, demeanor, service style, and personal approach before they were ready to invite strangers into their home.

Their concept of church renewal was to have more people come and help pay the bills They didn't want to do anything to welcome those strangers in. They didn't want to make friends with them if they came. And they didn't want to change anything they were already doing, things which hadn't worked for forty years already. Growth was a fruitless proposition.

They suggested we just change the name of the church and keep doing what we were doing already. A new name change was all it would take to draw the folks in, so they thought. My family and I discussed this around the dinner table one night. My two high school daughters sang on the worship team with me. There actually weren't any additional members to the worship team, just us.

The youngest one spoke up suggesting, "How about, 'Toon-Town Covenant Church'?" It was an appropriate suggestion.

After four months of being there I showed the pastor and board that the church was consistently burning through its money to the tune of a $15,000 a month deficit spending. Their two-to-three-year plan was only going to last another ten months before the entity was broke – they panicked.

At that point, I suggested they had two choices: A) Sell the building and move to the suburbs like everyone else or, perhaps, B) Do something radical and reach out to the existing neighborhood, because young families from the suburbs weren't going to come down to that part of town to join a church anyway. They opted to sell.

Several of them felt that they were sitting on a real-estate gold mine and all they had to do was put it on the market and then drift lazily into a blue-sky future on a golden parachute. After all, that's what the nice Lutherans next door had done.

We brought in a specialist for church sites who informed us it would take two years to sell and the church group would get half what the building had been worth only a year or two before, because of the economic downturn. The congregation looked pale and sick, more than usual.

Right after that, some of them decided to fire the senior pastor who had only bought the parsonage seven months earlier. There was a big fight, of course, and when the dust settled we decided to lay-off the unnecessary support staff, reduce program budgets, and restructure the pastor's role and pay. I became the lead and he became the associate with a new position and job responsibilities. The entire board stepped down and a new one was elected. Several people who hated the pastor left because they couldn't get him fired. He quit a few months later anyway then a bunch more folks who loved him left, blaming me. So, in the end, we had endured a lot of unnecessary drama and gone through a savagely brutal fight to get to nothing.

On January 1, 2010, I became the solo pastor of a dysfunctional, downtown, urban church without support staff and with a limited budget. There was no secretary, no janitor, not one single other paid position; there were few volunteers. But we bought ourselves one more year of time to try and do something to revitalize the church and stay alive. Maybe we would find a cure for our zombie condition. We had one thing going for us, a ministry we'd started just four months earlier.

7. CHILI AND CORNBREAD

We had struggled throughout 2009 (with so many problems that were just plain ridiculous but kept us mired in quicksand and mud) trying to pull the cart free from the ruts of the past. When the dust settled on the big fight over the senior pastor, and we knew we couldn't sell the building, I knew we had to do something quick to bring change.

The older pastor's new title was Pastor of Compassion and Social Justice Ministries. He claimed this was his true heart's calling. I wanted him to create an outreach community meal for the poor, but he wanted to launch a recovery ministry instead. So, beginning September 1st, 2009, he focused all his time and energy into a Wednesday night recovery group for the next ten weeks. At the end of the ten weeks no one was coming to the recovery group. It had two people from outside the church that he recruited to help him launch the ministry and that was it. No one else had come. That's what helped him decide to resign.

In early September, the same time the former pastor was trying to get his recovery group off the ground, my wife and I turned our attention to the community meal. On a wet Monday night in 2009, she and I put together a huge vat of chili and several sheets of cornbread. While she put the finishing touches on the meal and got the gym ready, I walked the back alleys and side streets of the neighborhood with a little flyer I made inviting every addict, prostitute, downtrodden, browbeaten, lonely soul I could find to come to the church for a free meal and to watch Monday Night Football with us.

My little flyer said, "Come on in for a Free Meal and Monday Night Football for the Neighborhood." It also listed three rules everyone was to follow: 1) Don't come high or drunk, 2) Be polite, and, 3) Don't ask for money. They drifted in by twos and threes. They came in cautious and wary, like zebras at the lion's favorite watering hole. Some of them acted nervous and skittish, like they thought they would get hit by lightning or worse yet, pounced on by a pamphlet-wielding Bible-thumper. They finally settled in at the various round tables scattered across the gym floor and settled in to watch the game. Football is a great conversation starter and community builder.

One lady walked up to me and introduced herself, asking me exactly who I was.

"I'm the pastor here," I assured her as I stood there wearing blue jeans, a sweatshirt, and a baseball cap.

"I couldn't believe it when you came around passing out that flyer inviting us to come to this place for a meal. I've been homeless down here for ten years and this church never does nuthin' for nobody."

"Well I'm here now and maybe between you and me together we can change all that?!" I didn't know it then, but she would later become a friend of mine. She and her heroin addict boyfriend would help me paint my office. The two of them would later drift into church, have an experience with Jesus, and get a life back. But this first night it was all about free food, football, and introductions.

I stood by the entryway door for a while greeting everyone that came in.

One guy asked me doubtfully, "You're the pastor? I've eaten meals in churches all over town and I've never met a pastor before!" He made the announcement like a carnival barker telling a contestant they'd just won a stuffed animal. He stuck out his big dirty paw and said, "Put 'er there pastor!" He vigorously shook my whole arm the whole while. I took note of that comment and marked it in my mind for future reference. When ministry is done among the homeless I guess it isn't being done by pastors.

One giant Native American guy staggered in drunk as a skunk, barely able to stand, all his words were totally slurred to the point of being barely understandable. He overheard me introducing myself as the pastor, so he sloshed up to me and stood there like a tree half cut through in a windstorm. "Pashur, I'm-a rea-y to re-ded-ish-cashe my lives to da Lard," He managed to get out.

You're ready to rededicate your life to the Lord? You're ten feet in the door, without hearing a prayer or song or sermon or nothing and slobbery drunk to boot," I thought to myself. I doubted his sincerity. I looked him up and down and in an instant, I knew exactly what he thought was going on. I would later over many, many conversations get my first impression verified.

This group of people is used to Christians coming down to their neighborhood park or to their spot under the freeway to give out sandwiches and coats and such. But almost always these free gifts come with a price. The price is hearing a sermon, or listening to a worship team, or getting a tract read to you, or other such performance driven marketing tools being thrust upon the poor and homeless *before* a meal can be eaten or a coat can be worn. Usually the team loads back up on the van, bus, or truck and doesn't come back until next month, or more often, next year.

We saw this quite a lot in our neighborhood, especially at Thanksgiving and Christmas. Do-gooder Christians come out of the woodwork at those times, twice a year when it's seasonally fashionable to care about the poor, then they disappear. They, just like the average folk go to church at Christmas and Easter and think it suffices; Christians help the poor at Thanksgiving and Christmas and think it's enough.

If the poor, homeless, drug addicts pretend to pray a conversion prayer and get "saved," they often, then, tap the sappy, believe-everything-ya-tell-them-do-gooder-Christians with a sob story of hardship, then score an extra sandwich, get another blanket for their non-existent girlfriend who is "too sick to come down here," or score money for supposed prescription medications that they can't afford but which will save their lives.

I swear my first four months doing this kind of thing every fourth person I met was diagnosed with cancer. After the Christians load up in their bus and drive away the homeless laugh and mock at what naïve saps these guys are, then spend the time gloating, showing off what they scored from them while wishing and hoping they come back next week too.

The gospel has become a con game. This is what the homeless in our area usually think; *I pretend to accept your Jesus and I get extra stuff from you. But you Christians have no intention of having me in your church or inviting me to your home for a Bible study or being my friend. I've never had a Christian ever take the time to simply ask me my life story or want to be my friend or care about my opinions or insights. It's all just a push to get people converted with the use of a pamphlet or tract and then back to the suburbs. But you actually don't care about any of us as people.*

I saw all that in the drunken native's slurred proclamation. He even knew the right church-insider lingo, for crying out loud! How many dedications and rededications do you suppose had he been through?

I looked up at him and patted him on the shoulder and said gently, "Hey man there's one thing we really don't like around here and its religious hypocrites. You don't have to be one here. Just come on in and get warm, have some free food and enjoy the football. If you ever really want to talk about God, sometime in the future, let me know." He staggered off bewildered and confused because this isn't the way the game is played and clearly, I didn't know the rules. But I've always been a rule breaker.

During the commercials, I turned down the TV and gave away gloves, blankets, and hats and such using trivia questions. I had one sports question, one Bible question, and one general history or knowledge question. It was fun. Fun is something I found out they almost *never* get anywhere. My wife and I thought that we would hold the meal and watch football and in the process of getting to know them we would discern what kind of ministry to start. It turned out this neighborhood community meal *was* the ministry. We built camaraderie and respect and made friendships fast.

After that first night, we only had two rules; Be polite and don't ask for money (because we didn't have any). They were polite too. Even drunk or high they stayed polite and well behaved. The church became their sanctuary, their place of safety, their territory, their home base. Very quickly beer cans and needles became less scattered around the church. I would sit across the street at Starbucks on some mornings and watch homeless guys go around the church grounds picking up trash to make the place nicer. It was their way of showing respect.

I frequently told them at the meals that this is still God's house, so it gets to be a place where all grudges are left at the door and all problems from the street don't get brought in here to break out in a fist fight or cussing match. Whatever has gone on outside it needs to stay out there. In the gym it was peace, safety, and protection for all, even though it's just a brief time. "Sanctuary for all" we called it. If you can't handle that then you would have to leave. I had guys who had been in knife fights with each other earlier in the week sit a couple of tables away from each other and keep peace.

Over the next five years we would continue this meal. Eventually we created a separate non-profit corporation apart from the church to get donations to help with the costs of this enterprise. We called this ministry STREET WISE. We didn't know it then, but we would find ourselves raising up to $40,000 a year through this ministry and it would be the only thing to save the church, in the end.

Little by little, the neighborhood folks began to trust us and one by one started coming to church services on Sunday mornings. Boy, did that start to change things.

8. CHURCH RULES

We were a trashy run down old building in an urban blight neighborhood. The juniper bushes around the church were overgrown and wildly twisted with years of wind and the lack of a decent trim job. The ground was mostly overgrown weeds and many of the windows had been broken out and boarded up because it was cheaper than replacing the glass.

When my daughters told friends at school where they sang in church, the reply was often, "That building is still open? I thought it was closed down years ago!"

We didn't have any money, so I did the best I could and tried to come up with a cheap advertising campaign that turned our hideous eyesore into some kind of an asset. I hoped to show that we were still alive despite how we looked. We took pictures of some of our younger members and their kids, in all kinds of action or social interaction settings and we made two big full color banners for two-sides of the church with their pictures plastered all over the banners. One banner on the main drag of Division Street read:

> Don't Judge a Church by Its Cover
> Like a Person, It's What's Inside That Counts!

The other one across the street from Starbucks said,

> Don't Be Fooled by Our Building
> We're Not Your Mama's Church!

We didn't have very good church signage at the time, so few people knew our name; for the next couple of years when I would meet people and describe where I worked they would say, "Oh you're - Not your mama's church!" Yeah, that's us.

When the homeless started to attend church services we really lived up to that reputation. We definitely were NOT your Mama's church. We had the two rules: "Be Polite, Don't Ask for Money." But now we realized, for church to run smoothly, we had to add a few more rules to the list: "Please don't hide your beer in the toilet tanks to keep them cold during services," was one of the new rules. Another was, "If you like something the pastor says in the sermon you don't have to call out, 'That's right pastor, Kick the demons in the A**' - a hearty 'Amen' will suffice." Also, "Please keep your knives securely folded and stored in your bags" and "Leave personal fingernail grooming to another time," was another rule we needed to add.

One day, when I was done leading worship and getting ready to speak, a guy slid over next to me in the pew during the announcements and offering time and in a grizzly bear's voice he rasped, "Ya got any smokes?"

"No, I don't," I firmly but politely replied.

"You ain't got no smokes for me?" He asked with squinty little distrusting eyes doubting my sincerity. A look of confusion came over his face for just an instant and then he added accusingly, "You up there playing the gee-tar ain't ya?"

"Yes"

"Well you gave me smokes, last week!" he practically shouted.

"Will you keep your voice down," I hushed him strongly while the announcements moved on without a moment's pause. In my strongest whisper I told him, "I did not give you smokes last week. Are you sure it wasn't that other guy over there?" I pointed out a grizzled old fellow with long shaggy gray hair and a bushy gray beard who wasn't homeless himself but lived in a trailer, and sure could blend in with the downtown crowd without a single minor addition or subtraction. He had been helping me out by playing back up guitar and harmony vocals for a few months.

The old guy peered at him with his squinty gaze and responded like a witness at a line up.

"Yeah I guess it was *him* gave me the smokes".

I was relieved that he had come to his senses and now knew the error of his ways; since I keep an extremely short haircut and don't look a thing like that other musician. I decided to write down right there on the spot another rule for the church to live by, "Please do not ask the pastor for smokes during church services!"

One day an extremely dirty, wild-haired, crazy man came into the church about two minutes before the start of service. He was carrying an old beat-up guitar on his back. I was praying over in the area, which we call The Prayer Loft, trying to get myself spiritually ready for the blessing of the Lord that I knew would fall on me this day if I just prepared my heart properly. I warily watched him come in and settle into a pew about half way back on the center aisle.

We only had one usher in those days, a delightful man well into his seventies who stands about five feet five and is one of the nicest guys you will ever meet, but he wasn't a very good bouncer. So, I glanced around the room to measure up whom else I might I call upon if needed to heed the ministry of Jesus today. But there was no one who looked bulked up enough to assist in the work of God I could sense coming.

Had I been more aware I would have recognized this man as the one who came in one Sunday many weeks before after we had just put up our advertising signs. He stomped in from the outdoors and stood in the lobby at the back of the sanctuary and shouted at me while I was doing announcements that his own sweet dear mother *did indeed* attend this church in the past and I could "Shove it, you goddam yuppie pastor," then he stormed out. So, the "Not Your Mama's Church" ad campaign wasn't successful with everyone. We stopped the announcements and prayed for him and then moved on with the service.

Now, unbeknownst to me, he was back. He looked comfortable and calm, so I returned to my devotional prayers before the Lord. Suddenly I heard a loud TWANG, TWANG, TWANG from his aggressive strumming on the electric strings put on his acoustic guitar which were badly in need of a tuning at that. "JIMMY PAGE, JIMMY PAGE!" He shouted at the top of his lungs in counter point to the rhythm he strummed.

My reverence was broken. I marched in long strides right up to him in the center aisle and put my finger in his face and announced "HEY YOU – NOT HERE! NOT NOW! NOT TODAY!"

"Oh yeah" he retorted, "Well then F*%&# YOOOUUUUU!" he shouted. He grabbed his gear and stormed out.

I looked around the room at the big eyes staring at me from every pew in every corner. "Well it's not your standard call to worship," I thought to myself, "but I guess today we'll have to go with it."

I found out later that he was a diagnosed schizophrenic and he was a child of the church, too. His mother was one of the last remaining godly saints in our midst. She could pray like nobody's business. And my heart broke for her. What saintly mother ever holds a newborn babe and hopes that the child grows up to be a wild and violent, homeless, mentally ill, man wandering the streets aimless, purposeless and friendless. I've prayed for them both many times.

One guy started coming on a regular basis who used to deal a lot of drugs. He had once been one of Spokane's biggest meth cookers. He claimed to be deeply connected to a lot people who would be very embarrassed if it ever got out that they were users. He really liked me and the church and wanted to make whatever contribution he could to help. He was now clean and sober (or so he claimed) and was trying to get his life restarted. He came up to me one day and glancing over both shoulders leaned toward me and in a conspiratorial whisper said, "If you ever need anyone disappeared around here I could arrange that for you with one or two phone calls," as he gave me an affirmative nod of conviction.

I was a bit stunned to say the least. Here I was a long term committed Christian pastor leading a 125-year-old church, trying to drag it from a dead past into a vibrant future, retooling and reengineering all its ministries, all the while doing it under the stress and duress of serving a unique homeless population while trying to keep my own cool and sanity. I asked for his business card.

9. PREACHING GOOD NEWS TO THE ZOMBIFIED

We kept doing the meals but on Super Bowl Sunday, 2010, we moved them from Monday nights to Sunday afternoons and kept them in that time slot. Part of the reason for this was that on Mondays my wife and I did all the cooking and setting up all afternoon and when other volunteers got off work they came down to just dish out the food. We were being overwhelmed with the labor and thought we might get some better volunteer help on Sunday afternoons in preparing the meals. We were right.

The other reason is that we finally corrected a typical, yet common and crucial mistake we church people do when we start a ministry to the poor. We didn't do any homework with anyone already in the neighborhood to discover what was already being done and how we could supplement or assist existing works. I don't know why churches do this, but we always seem to feel it's the call of God on our ministry to save the world single handedly. We learned there was another Monday night meal already in existence and a few other churches downtown served other days of the week. Nobody was serving a meal on Sundays, so we took that time slot. All of us who were preparing and distributing meals got so connected we advertised each other's meals and often shared surplus goods. One of those ministries ended up losing its location to serve the meals and contracted with us to offer a meal out of our building on Thursday nights. We agreed.

The meals weren't supposed to be our ministry. They were supposed to teach us what kind of ministry to build but we were few in number. Many, many weeks and months there was a kitchen crew but only myself and one other Christian guy in the room trying to represent for Jesus among the 150-200 street people coming in. I was in way over my head and way over any training I'd ever had.

I've had some pretty wild discussions with people about their lives and God. One woman I met told me how she hated God because her ex-husband was building a meth lab in their house while she had gone to work. The cops raided the place and arrested her because the lease was in her name. She did time in prison and while there, the ex-husband beat their six-year-old child to death. She hates God for not protecting her little girl. She is a drug addict and has had another child taken away by Child Protective Services because of her habit. She had been recently diagnosed with a major illness, but they wouldn't treat her while she's using drugs. Before our talk ended she asked me if I would pray for her and that other baby girl out there somewhere. Despite her fears and hatred of God, we did.

Another man told me about how he punched a guy out at a nightclub in an argument over his wife. He talked of wanting to change but not being able. We talked of sin, God, righteousness and coming to the place where we all realize we can't become the men or women we really want to be on our own. Sooner or later we all realize that we need God's grace to change. I gave him a Bible and told him to read the Gospel of John. He and his wife started coming to church regularly after that. She told me he was changing since meeting Jesus.

I took a van load of hand-picked homeless guys to my daughter's high school musical play once. When afterwards I was dropping them off at the shelter where they live, the directions consisted of, "Turn right at the prostitute on the corner, left into the alley between these two old buildings, and stop where it looks like those two guys are making a drug deal."

Getting out of the van one guy laughed and said, "Want us to write those directions down for next time Pastor Rob?"

The last guy to exit turned back to me and said in quiet tones, "Thanks for reminding us that there is another life out there, Pastor Rob." At the time, that guy was trying to get his Class C driver's license back and planned on reentering the mainstream of life.

There are so many stories. Sometimes all that is needed for some is a friend to share the hope of Christ and believe in them again. On any given Sunday afternoon or Thursday night a Christian man or woman can get into a half dozen discussions, when we feed the poor at our church. I mostly focused on the Sundays and let that other organization work with its team in our building on Thursdays. But many a Sunday there were only four or five us Christians in the room amidst the 150-200 poor people who came in. That's an awfully light witness.

I'm always amazed that the Bible speaks so much about our Christianity impacting the poor but so few of us have any kind of track record doing it. Jesus said of his mission, "The Spirit of the Lord is on me, because he has anointed me to preach good news to the poor. He has sent me to proclaim freedom for the prisoners and recovery of sight for the blind, to release the oppressed." (Luke 4:18, NASB)

Years ago, when I worked at a large church that ran a $1.4 million annual budget, I would often read verses about the poor and get a cold chill up my spine. We did very little for the poor while we ran our huge program and spent the money on our staff and facility. I often wondered how much of our efforts would burn when Jesus came back.

James 1:27 says, "Pure and undefiled religion in the sight of our God and Father is this: to visit orphans and widows in their distress, and to keep oneself unstained by the world." (NASB) I guess my religion in those days was pretty impure and much defiled. I'm not sure how I'd measure it now.

If you are ever haunted that your faith might be just a sham full of a lot of pretentious activity, maybe you ought to try living out the commands to minister to the poor. Go down to any meal, or outreach somewhere. See if Jesus has a divine appointment scheduled for you! Take a chance and see if the Holy Spirit will use your life. You'll be in over your head, but very glad you did.

10. GOD HUNTS US DOWN FOR ANOTHER CHANCE

Katie walked into our church the last Sunday of May 2010, dazed, confused, and scared. On the Thursday night prior, she had gotten into an argument with her mom, because she didn't want to take an eight-week summer camp job her mom had lined up for her. The argument ended with her mom informing her that she had fifteen minutes to pack her things and get out or she would call the cops and have her eighteen-year-old daughter thrown out. An hour later, mom dropped her off at homeless shelter downtown, driving away with the parting words, "Have a nice life."

Katie found herself checking into a shelter for homeless women, many of whom are hardcore meth or heroin addicts, prostitutes, or suffering severe mental disorders. She had nothing but a small school backpack and two plastic grocery bags full of clothes. That was her welcome into the adult world!

Katie is the biological product of a prostitute in San Francisco. She and her brother were adopted as young children by a couple where the father was the main care giver and the mother the main bread winner. In their teen years, the father unexpectedly died leaving mom to care for Katie, her brother, and two other young children they had also adopted. The mom was estranged from her own family and extended relatives. She had been unable to build strong relationships with the father's side either, so mom up and moved the family out of state to a remote area north of Spokane, WA.

Mom did this without consulting or conferring with the children, nor did mom notify the extended relatives of the move. When they arrived they had no family, no friends, or connections in this state. Mom felt she could financially provide in a cheaper area and it seemed she wanted to get away from California.

Katie and her brother begrudgingly enrolled in the high school where Katie made just a few friends in her two months there. The grief, conflicts, anger, and rebellion Katie had against the situation caused so much hostility in the home that mom shipped her off to a reform school in Utah. Katie stayed there for the next two years.

Katie worked through many of her personal issues during that time with counseling, support and professional help. A few weeks before her 18th birthday mom had Katie sent back home against the school's recommendations and against Katie's own desires. At home, the conflicts with mom remained unresolved.

So now, a few days after her eighteenth birthday, mom gave Katie fifteen minutes to pack and get out. She drove her to downtown and dumped her off. Katie wandered the streets for a few days lost and alone in a place where she had no family, friends, or support structure of any kind.

At that time, we had a volunteer soundman that was a homeless person himself. He turned out to be a pathological liar and a thief, but he was, hands down, our best inviter. On a Sunday morning sitting at the local Catholic Charities homeless shelter he approached her, took one look at her said, "You don't belong here."

He invited her to our church since many of the local homeless attended our services. Not knowing where else to turn, frightened and alone, Katie came to a church service of her own volition for the first time in her life. Prior to this moment she had never set foot in a church except for a wedding or funeral.

When she walked in the doors she nearly broke down in tears. Up on the stage rehearsing for the worship that day were my teen daughters, the only two high school kids in our whole church. They just happened to be two of the few friends Katie had made more than two years earlier in a high school located twelve miles away.

What are the odds that she would walk into a downtown urban church with only two high school kids in the congregation, in a state she'd barely lived in, in which she had no extended family, and then, for her very first church service, find a known friend? That was God watching out for her.

They all three fell on each other laughing and crying, Katie with relief. She stayed through the service, helped in the kitchen with our feeding program and then we took her home with us for the next few weeks.

Not long after that, we were able to help get Katie into her own apartment. Through church support, we were able to get her furniture as well. She enrolled in one of the local community colleges and began to get stable in her life. She gave her life to Christ a few months later, was baptized in our church, and grew to become our Nursery and Preschool Director.

Her journey, even with Christ, wasn't the smooth easy straight path. There was a lot to overcome.

I have watched Katie grow and develop as a woman and a leader. Her starting point was so much lower than most people that I give her extra credit for how far she has come. She literally stood at a crossroads where her destiny could have been either a drug addicted stripper or prostitute, or she could overcome against all odds and establish herself as a productive, happy and fruitful person. God was intervening in her story saving her from that first alternative. It happened just because we happened to be in the right place at the right time.

In Summer 2012, Katie completed her Associate of Arts Degree and headed off to Seattle Pacific University (SPU) that fall. SPU is a Christian university where she planned on getting a degree in education or early childhood development. She planned on spending her life rescuing kids just like her.

Katie's story would keep unfolding in the years after. She had some dark paths ahead due to unresolved issues and it wouldn't turn out as any of us planned. I still to this day know God his hand on that girl in a special way that she doesn't even realize.

11. WHAT WOULD YOU SAY?

I found myself standing with a cup of coffee in a room full of street people some time ago thinking about Jesus' words. "The Spirit of the Lord is upon me, because he has anointed me to preach good news to the poor." Luke 4:18 *(NASB)*

I had to confess; I didn't really know what that meant anymore. After all my years of training, experience and education, somehow converting that phrase to, "Jesus loves you," didn't seem to have much punch. It can't be that, "He died on the cross for your sins," for that news is for everyone, not just the poor. *What is the good news for the poor?* Is it, "Don't worry the church has arrived to rescue you"? It doesn't look like it. I admit that I was, and still am, in a transitional time of my own life, reevaluating a lot of my own Christian experiences and assumptions. I just don't know what to say, really. Perhaps you are wiser than I am and can answer the question— *What is good news to the poor?*

I looked around the room and saw K, who has ovarian cancer. She's going to have a complete hysterectomy next month. She's in her early thirties. She has been saving up all her money for months to rent a rundown little hotel room for a week or two in order to recuperate in a bed with a roof over it. Her recent birthday money put her over the top. She told me she spent seventeen or eighteen years in two violently abusive relationships. She said life for her, those years, was like being stuck in a closet. She drank herself into oblivion to deal with the pain. Her family will have nothing to do with her but have set up a fund she can tap if she stays sober. She's been sober a while and is working on it, but lives on the street and the fear is always with her. "You have to be really careful as a woman out here," she whispers to me. She likes coming to church because people remember her name and say hi. So, tell me, what would you say to her? *What's the good news for K?*

T helps out around the church a lot. He was once a big-time drug user and manufacturer — "cooker," is what he called it. He had a plumber's license once but lost that and his driver's license when he went to jail on a drug bust. He lost his family, home and everything after that. No one in his life really knew what he was doing. His last drug drop ended up murdered and he was the last one to see the guy alive, so he had to leave town for a long time even though there was no further evidence against him. He wants to get his life back somehow but can't drive and has a bad back, so he can't do the plumbing anymore. He came to church for the first time in thirty years and likes it. *What's the good news for him? What would you say?*

I met B at one of our meals just a couple weeks before that. He has deep scars on his wrists for the many times he's tried to commit suicide. He admits to doing a lot of dope and to having been a cutter to cover the pain. Both his parents and one brother committed suicide so he's alone now. He tells me he doesn't believe in God since he went through a two-year span where fourteen of his friends and family died. Most of those were either killed in drunken driving accidents or committed suicide. He's in his twenties and lives on the streets now. *What would you say to him that's good news?*

R comes all the time. I've seen him so high he scares other people around him. His back was broken at the age of eight by an abusive dad, adding to his many scars. He watched his best friend blow his brains out playing Russian Roulette with what they thought was an empty gun. Turns out the boy's guardian had loaded the pistol knowing the teen liked to play that game with the empty gun. The guardian was tired of dealing with him and thought this would be an easy out. R has some mental issues as you could guess, but I like him. When he's clean and sober he's a good guy but paranoid. He'll talk to me though. He once tried to get off drugs by going to Union Gospel Mission and enrolling in Moody Bible Institute for a year. He's a tough street guy now. *What's the good news for him?*

R runs with D, who has three kids in Arizona somewhere living with other family members, because she couldn't take care of them due to drug use. At twelve she was abducted by three men and gang-raped for two days in the desert, beaten and left for dead. A neighbor-lady's dog found her. She's got a lot of memories like that but doesn't want to explore them to get any potential healing. She likes heroin for forgetting. She's been diagnosed as having multiple personalities, also known as Dissociative Identity Disorder. *What's the good news you'd share with her?*

J grew up in foster care until he was eight. He was adopted by an abusive family with several other older adopted boys who were all just as violent. He ran away at fourteen. He lived with another family in small town many miles north for a while but couldn't conform and eventually hit the streets. He's twenty-two and has been living on the streets for six years. He does drugs, has no education or skills, and still remembers the pain of growing up in a violent home. He doesn't tell his story to many people, "'cause what's the use? They don't care." He's come to church twice and likes it. *What is the good news for J?*

There were three of us, Christians, in the room that day among the poor people at our meal, each with a story similar to these. I stood around with my coffee and thought about how all my answers seemed so tiny in the scope of their lives. They will leave here fed but camping out somewhere in the shelters, alleys and back ways of the city.

I'm not sure what to say to them that really is good news and there weren't enough other Christians "representing" to bail me out. What did Jesus really mean when he said that? Perhaps you understand better what Jesus meant and you know exactly what to say. Maybe you should be the one here and not me.

SECTION 3: TRYING TO SURVIVE IN ZOMBIELAND

My brethren, do not hold your faith in our glorious Lord Jesus Christ with an attitude of personal favoritism. For if a man comes into your assembly with a gold ring and dressed in fine clothes, and there also comes in a poor man in dirty clothes, and you pay special attention to the one who is wearing the fine clothes, and say, 'You sit here in a good place,' and you say to the poor man, 'You stand over there, or sit down by my footstool,' have you not made distinctions among yourselves, and become judges with evil motives? Listen, my beloved brethren: did not God choose the poor of this world to be rich in faith and heirs of the kingdom which He promised to those who love Him?

James 2:1-5 (NASB)

12. I GUESS I'M CRAZY

I've read about how poor downtown churches should partner with big affluent ones to survive. After many months of running our meals I met a guy from a big church who is their staff person responsible for local outreach. They wanted to work with street kids in the downtown area. He came with a team to see what we were doing, and they expressed a desire to partner with us.

The idea hatched to create a Tuesday afternoon or evening event for the street kids under the age of twenty-five using our facility and their people. I introduced their team to some of our street kids who gave them tons of ideas. "How crazy", I thought, "these irreligious, runaway, street-kids are begging for ministry and their ideas are GREAT! This could be good."

"Okay", I told him, "but remember we are a very small and extremely poor church. We only have about sixty people and a third of them are homeless. We can't afford to underwrite or financially sustain the ministries of your huge church".

"Don't worry about that," he laughed dismissively; "You won't be financially carrying us".

We created a plan for them to bring a team down every Tuesday for four to six hours. They would do recreational activities with the youth and develop educational and life goals with them all the while sharing the love of Jesus. We thought that asking for use of our facility's gym, kitchen, restrooms, and a couple of breakout rooms would work nicely. Our board decided that asking $150 a night from them was fair, since we cover the paper towels, toilet paper, water bill, cleaning supplies, dumpster fees, etc. Our heat bill alone is $2,000 or more a month in the winter months so their entire fee wouldn't cover even a third of that cost. But it would be a great help to us. He put a plan together and submitted it to his board who then asked to pray about it. Over the next month, no one called, no one visited, and no one came to investigate.

He called me some six weeks later. "They don't like the idea of paying that much money to only use your facility four times a month." he said matter-of-factly.

Having priced downtown real estate I thought that $115 a night to use several thousand-square feet for four to six hours, wasn't unreasonable, it was actually a DEAL! Had he said, "We can't afford it at this time," or, "We just aren't ready to pursue the total costs of taking on this project," or "Our missions budget is tapped, could we only come twice a month?" Then, I would've been fine. But I was a bit ruffled by his words.

"I'm sure that your church charges a lot more when renting out its facility for weddings," I retorted. I found out later they charge $450 for four hours use of just one room, $100 more for each additional hour. Janitorial and other fees are on top of that. But, I admit, their place in the suburbs is much nicer than ours.

There was a long pause on the phone. "That's not ministry," he said; "We're trying to help street kids," he answered in a tone implying I was an evil, greedy, scamming preacher who should be on TV.

I didn't want to get sidetracked discussing whether a marriage union before the Lord God Almighty in His holy church constituted an act of ministry, so I said, "Remember when I told you that our little church wasn't able to support or underwrite the ministry of your huge, rich church? This is what I meant. We just can't pay for you guys to do your ministry here."

He told me they aren't a rich church. I suppose it's because their cash flow is tied up in multiple staff salaries, benefits, massive facilities, huge program budgets, major equipment purchases, and overseas mission trips.

As our conversation continued I began to resent his implications that we aren't about the kingdom because we didn't *give* them our facility to do this ministry; although the double standard of them charging for their facility didn't seem to bother him.

Am I crazy? I suppose I am. I'm learning what partnering with big churches means; they tap our location and the good relationships we've built with the homeless community, we give them our facility for free to do their ministry, and we pick up the overhead costs. In exchange, they give us . . . Well, um, . . *nothing*. They decided not to do ministry with street kids here. Call me crazy but I think the world is upside down. I think a tiny downtown church of sixty people, some of whom are homeless and poor, shouldn't be asked to pick up the tab of an affluent church of several thousand attendees from one of the richest neighborhoods in town.

I had thought a big affluent church would be excited to support and help sustain the urban work of a downtown church full of poor people. Boy, did I get that wrong. Too bad for the street kids though. I've often wondered if I'm the only one who is crazy.

13. LOOKING UP AT THE UNDERBELLY OF THE AMERICAN CHURCH

"Legions of fruitless followers paying the bills." I heard that phrase from the lips of my pastor friend as we sat around a table during a pastor's prayer luncheon. We were lamenting the change of life we had both experienced in ministry. Things were so much easier when we were in the big corporate church with multi-levels of pastoral staff; each specializing in a specific role. Now we were both in struggling downtown churches with small congregations in dirt poor neighborhoods.

"Yes," he said, "I miss the days when legions of fruitless followers gathered and paid the bills."

What a perfect phrase for some of my own experiences! I had to confess that I missed it too. It was nice in the big church to focus on one or two roles and be a specialist as, numerous others took care of areas of ministry or business which never once crossed my mind or my plate! Things are so much harder now in a tiny church as a solo pastor with no support staff. Even what I'm really good at I can't do as well because there is not enough time to specialize. But we both admitted that being on the front lines battling poverty, loneliness, despair, and hopelessness is a lot closer to

Biblical Christianity than sitting in the affluent church. We both thought this is where Jesus would be if he were to come to our town in the flesh. But we both missed the ease and the accolades of being in the big church. *(Sigh)*

On any given Sunday— right here in the greater Spokane area; thousands of Christians will gather in hundreds of churches. Millions of dollars will be collected in the name of Christ just this Sunday alone. Countless hours of sermons will be preached, thousands of hours of Sunday school and Bible study will occur this week.

Do you have any idea what all those thousands of people and millions of dollars and hundreds of hours of teaching and study will produce for the poorest, most destitute, most broken and lost people in our downtown? What the direct benefit was to the hundred or more people who wandered into our church for a meal? . . . . Not very much.

Volunteers of America was in the neighborhood, Catholic Charities, and a few liberal groups were all down here working but the Evangelical, Bible-believing, Jesus-following, relationship-proclaiming churches had little effect on those 150 people who walked into our church.

Any given Sunday we would have a room full of some of the most broken, lost, wounded, hurting people in our town. Six or seven Christians would be cooking and serving in our kitchen and another four or five more would be mixing among the poor and homeless, praying, laughing, joking, encouraging and sharing the love of Jesus. Only ten Christians, maybe twelve. That's all there usually were in total.

The funds to produce this meal came from friends outside of our church, mostly out of state people. A business leader who is a board member from another church in town sent his monthly check to help. Numerous friends of my wife's and mine who still lived in California, Chicago, and Arizona would give the majority of the financial support for our meals. The mega-church, two miles away, who just finished a lengthy series on helping the poor last fall was represented once or twice for a while — by *two* people.

Looking up at the under belly of the American church from down here at the bottom of the world was changing my faith. I keep hearing that there are churches who want to help the poor, but I didn't really see it.

First Covenant is located on a main intersection of the busiest street in town. We were two blocks away from the only interstate within several hundred miles. Given our location I'm sure every single one of those churches that wanted to help has board members and pastors who have driven right past us in the last several months and never once stopped or called to see if there's something going on.

It's the story of the Good Samaritan in real life. While we lay there on the side of the Jericho road struggling to stay alive the priests and Levites passed by daily, never once stopping.

The Volunteers of America, Spokane Neighborhood Action Program, Gonzaga Campus Kitchen, Feed Spokane, and even Providence Health Care stopped by; Samaritans by any Evangelical standard of definition. Pastors, deacons, elders, Bible teachers, and small group leaders kept driving by on their way to study what it is Jesus wanted them to do.

I've spent most of my life as one of those, drive-by-Christians. I've spent time in comfortable roles at affluent churches. Now that I found myself down here looking up, I know that I should have added more action to my practice of faith.

Jesus said that he came "to preach good news to the poor". In truth, I've spent most my Christian life preaching *no news* to the poor. I have so much to learn! *Maybe it's time for a change in how church works.*

---

14. BITING THE WRONG HAND

I wrote many articles for a monthly newsletter which are now appearing in some form in this book. But at that time, we struggled along trying to build a church out of the remnants of that old historic mess in that dilapidated and broken neighborhood. I'm an analyzer and synthesizer by nature. My creative mind simply must find ways to examine situations assess the needs and explore ideas for possible outcomes and solutions to whatever systemic problem exists.

In this case I was wrestling with how to build an effective church in such a place and under such conditions. We were failing at church even if we were doing well at ministry.

I couldn't get people to come. We couldn't build any effective outreach programs to people of substance who would come and support the work with tithes and talents. Our church was losing money heavily and burning through the last remainder of the parsonage sale money no matter what I tried to do to stop the blood flow.

I became quite the real estate entrepreneur. We found ways to raise monthly cash flow by renting extra unused rooms to jazz bands for rehearsal space. I had contracts with a parking company to get revenue off our parking lot, but had to come up with a striping plan to add 20 spaces. We rented ourselves out to weekly events for other non-profits who wanted to use our prime location for outreach to the poor. I was constantly finding ways to generate revenue through use of office space or rental of our facility, but it was never enough. At one point, we were bringing in more than $2,000 a month from rental space alone. But it seemed like no matter how many contracts I negotiated, drafted, and signed it was never enough. For every contract I gained, we seemed to lose that much in giving. It was climbing uphill on a sand dune.

At one point, I thought the only solution for a downtown urban church is for a local mega-church or denomination to take on the facility and work with the poor. Either of those would have the thousands of people and hundreds of thousands of dollars of income (millions more likely) that could take on the finances of the building, hire a location pastor to do outreach and send their people down to the urban location to hand out food, give away blankets, pass out hats and gloves, befriend the poor, and share their stories of faith and hope.

A denomination could have several outlying suburban churches adopt an inner-city church as their mission outpost project. Either way when the mega-church or denomination talked to their people about the poor, they could say: "Go down there to our guy in the trenches. That's where we do it, that's where the work is sustained and that's where we connect you to your local poverty scene."

With that in mind, and because our church was running out of money so fast we only had less than a year of life, I emailed a local large-church pastor whom I had met to consider taking one hundred, or so, of their people and seeding a congregational work in our location. We were dead in the water anyway and I was planning on moving on to do something else with my life.

Usually, when you contact a large-church pastor you get no response. When you do, it often takes several months to make personal contact and set up a meeting. That's what I was expecting. To my surprise, he got back to me right away and set up a meeting within the week. They were good at church planting, so I was hoping the conversation would be about them peeling off a group of their folks who cared about ministry to the poor and incubate something in our dying facility, and I would move on. But he was coming to set me straight.

He was nice and kind and all, but there was some kind of tension in the air I couldn't figure out. He brought his full-time ministry associate whose job was to find ministries to plug their people into for outreach works of social justice and poverty. It was one of those conversations where you know you're talking about a subject, but you have the distinct impression that the other person has an entirely different aim or agenda for the meeting, but you can't figure out what it is. I have a habit to keep on talking, hoping to stumble upon whatever the real deal is; sometimes it works, sometimes it backfires.

At one point in the conversation I was asked rather directly what kind of training I intended to provide for their people so that they would be prepared to minister to the poor if they came down here. I kind of snapped inside at that point, but I stayed cool on the outside.

My head was reeling. This guy had a paid staff almost as big as my entire church. He had a full-time person who was sitting right beside him whose only job was to place their people in works of charity, but he wanted me to do the training for his people. *My wife and I didn't get no stinkin-trainin'! ...Badges? We don't got no stinkin' badges! We just showed up and got moving.*

Nowadays, if someone asked me I could cover a couple hours worth of information about all I've learned about poverty people and poverty culture, but I still wouldn't call that training—wisdom and knowledge gained by experience—but not really training.

Since the resignation of the former pastor, and my assuming full leadership as a solo pastor, my duties included sermon preparation and preaching, counseling, service planning, worship leading, creative arts and video preparation, band rehearsals, brochure and bulletin production, business management, board meetings, record keeping of those meetings, computer repair and maintenance, janitorial oversight, leadership for feeding 150 (plus) homeless people per week, office management, crisis counseling, oversight of building maintenance, copy machine work, purchase of all office supplies and ministry related materials, building relationships with the businesses and social services community around us, grant writing, fund raising, contract negotiating, and developing outreach and church growth strategies.

My wife had offered to help me since I was the lone employee of the church. She volunteered some thirty to forty hours per week in the church office, along with her duties as coffee ministry coordinator, nursery leader, kitchen manager, and supply procurer for the homeless feeding program.

Since the worship team consisted of only me and my guitar, my two teenage daughters singing, my thirteen-year-old son on the sound board, and one other couple (one of whom plays percussion, the other who runs PowerPoint up in the booth), I had begun to consider worship rehearsal as quality family time.

He was asking me to add *training his people to work with the poor* to my plate. There was an implication hanging in the air that these two were assessing whether our ministry was worthy of their blessing, based on whether I was an incompetent and unprepared leader. I didn't lean in, I leaned back.

Taking a deep breath I slowly and deliberately explained, "Well, Pastor, I think that if your people have been attending your church and listen to you preach every week for the last three or four years, if they've been attending their small group which you encourage them to join, and if they've been studying the Bible every week in someone's living room for the last year or two, and if they've taken any of the many classes or workshops your church offers then—*they're trained.*" I finished a touch dramatic. The conversation ended shortly thereafter.

On the way out the door, while standing on the steps of our church the last thing he said to me was, "You need to learn not to bite the hand that feeds you."

I thought those were strange words from a pastor whose church had not given us a single dime to buy so much as one Styrofoam coffee cup. But my brain wasn't working very well at the moment, because all I could think of was my friend Mike in Arizona who was financing us. Mike had been through a very bad divorce and was living in his parent's basement at midlife while he tried to rebuild himself. He was working as a computer tech but also had a side business selling *Dirty Banana Drink Mix* (a banana chocolate concoction) to the bars and strip clubs in Vegas. He was our biggest financial contributor at the time. I was never sure how to even pray for that one. A couple of this large church pastor's small groups had served in our meals many months earlier and given us some money for the meals, but Mike alone had given us three to four times the amount of those contributions combined. I just smiled confusedly, stood on the steps and waved goodbye as they drove off. I never spoke to them again.

I found out a few days later why he responded so quickly to meeting me. An associate staff member called me up extremely angry and read me the riot act over the phone over my newsletter article about *Looking Up at the Underbelly of the American Church*. At the time, my newsletter article went out to only sixty people, forty of whom lived out of state. Their staff had seen the newsletter article a few weeks prior and decided the whole thing was all about their church, which it wasn't—since I'd never worked at their church, *obviously.*

I'm sure I got that one wrong. Maybe Mike and I are all backwards. Maybe funding efforts that one believes in, that aren't very big, flashy, influential, or super-organized, are a waste. Maybe, all that Bible study and sermon listening isn't good enough. Maybe I should have created a training program for their people. Maybe just jumping and doing something, anything, even if you don't know what you're doing, is a terrible idea after all. But then again, what do I know? After all, . . . I'm crazy.

15. THE ACTUAL MISSION

Many years ago, I was in a church that jumped on the band wagon of having a "mission statement". It was the latest rage coming from the corporate world and churches were following suit. I guess we had forgotten why we existed and a cleverly assembled mission statement was the perfect solution.

After countless weeks and months of development, we put together a pithy two-sentence statement that was then put on posters and brochures and was promptly forgotten by most. The average person in our large church couldn't have recited it or identified it from numerous other sayings.

I noticed that we put the bulk of our emphasis, time, money, and staff hiring on the last three words: "...beginning with seekers." That meant: outreach events, evangelism strategies, and counting conversions and attendance records were the dominant forces behind everything we did. That's where the money got spent, the staff got hired and all purposes ended. That wasn't morally wrong, it was just lopsided and out of balance with the Bible.

Years later, after serving in several other churches and sitting through thousands of hours of board meetings, strategy sessions, team planning meetings, conferences, and training seminars, I came to the conclusion that the real, unspoken, and underlying mission statement of most of the churches I experienced was: *"We exist to get more people to come here, so that we could exist".*

I once wondered out loud, "If our church ceased to exist, who outside of our church would care?" In other words, it seemed we were totally self-serving. We existed only for those that we could benefit from if they stayed among us. But, if we disbanded, almost all these people would simply be absorbed into one of the numerous other churches doing pretty much the same thing and no one would even notice the absence after a year or so. Only those who attended received any benefit from our existence. It felt rather . . . well, selfish.

I was reminded of this when things weren't going very well financially for us. We were forced to put the building back up for sale. This was the second time we tried to sell it in my short time on staff. We were still under the advice that the market was bad, and it would take a while, but we were out of options.

I had been so ignorant about how to deal with poverty culture that I started attending meetings of the Spokane Homeless Coalition. It's a gathering of about fifty different agencies, government groups, non-profits and ministries that help the poor. Ours was the only church represented.

I was elected to the leadership three times – two of those were consecutive terms as chairman. I learned a lot and met a lot of other people who work among the poor. I began to create many partnerships with other agencies and groups, often using our wonderfully strategic location as a major center for works of health or distribution of essential needs items.

For about a two-year period, the Gonzaga Campus Kitchen held its weekly meal for the poor in our gym (on Thursday nights). Just after we put the site on the market, their leader came to me with tears in her eyes because she saw the for-sale signs go up on the building. Another woman who has worked for Spokane Neighborhood Action Program (SNAP) for many years confided in me that a bunch of the agency people had taken bets a long time ago about how long I'd last.

"You've made it more than twice as long as anyone thought," she told me. They've watched a lot of Christians come and go in this work. She used to be a Lutheran pastor's wife for many years and thought the church would toss me out, or I'd give up long before we got this far.

Numerous homeless people quietly came up to me almost in a state of panic and fear to ask, "How long before this all goes away?" When the homeless saw the for-sale signs their sorrow ran deep, but they are so accustomed to disappointment that their first reaction was to use their words and spend their time trying to console *me*, which I thought was really touching. Our church had become their place of hope and safety, and they were afraid it would all disappear—even though only a small percentage of them ever came to a church service, this was their home. "Like sanctuary," are the words that were most used. They experienced dignity, respect, and safety in our place.

A lady from another nonprofit told me at our last city-wide Coalition meeting that she wanted to look up my number to call me but couldn't remember the name of the church. Sticking her head out of her office at the shelter she works in, she called out "What's the name of that church where Pastor Rob . . . ", "FIRST COVENANT!" Came the chorus of replies from the poor gathered there before she even finished. *They know us.*

One Sunday afternoon as I was talking with a homeless drunk, I couldn't figure out why he was mad at me. Finally, through his slurred words he blurted out, "Because, everybody likes you! No matter where I go, from one end of town to the other, everyone here on the streets talks about you and how great you guys are and how much they like coming here."

Why would this anger him? In the end, it came out that he didn't think any of those people deserved it. I found that ironic. None of us do, but love shines through anyway.

That's the Mission of the church—GRACE! *God* knows what will come next. *He* loves the poor, so we keep going. *He* has answers for our future, as a collective and as individuals. We planned on holding on in faith until *He* leads us to what is next or just closed it all down and scattered us to new places.

"I guess we will just keep feeding the poor and destitute until we can't anymore" I had told a couple of pastors at a conference. We were out of solutions.

But now I know what it feels like to be in a church where there are way more people outside of our doors who care about our existence than there are inside. It feels good.

16. TIMING IS EVERYTHING

By the end of 2010 the church outreach to the poor was doing great, but the church itself was struggling and unable to remain solvent. In December, I sat down with two leaders and we did the math on our finances, determining we would be flat broke in late April of 2011 without so much as the ability to pay the garbage bill.

We had been trying to build the church against incredibly hostile odds, under-financed, under-manned, under-resourced, and under-skilled. My wife and I had been at it for over two years and couldn't get things to become stabilized and solid, let alone grow and increase enough to break even.

In December, we began to gently let the congregation know we weren't doing well and the end was coming soon. No one was surprised. They looked like the hometown fans being told you weren't making the playoffs after not winning a game all season. We would have to inevitably close the church down and go our separate ways. We couldn't run the money to the very end because we would need at least two months to officially close things down and get rid of the equipment and furnishings as we tried to sell the building off.

We had been in talks with our denominational leaders since the previous April on how to revitalize the church and how to buy time to make things happen. Nothing worked.

My prayer life doing ministry in California was, "Lord, please help us sell the building for five million dollars and buy the new site for ten million." And, he did.

Over the last year it had become, "Lord, please let my soundman make bail by Easter Sunday morning." He didn't.

Around that time, after church one day, one of our homeless people came up to me after service and asked, "So the church isn't doing very well, then?" This person was a kind and helpful soul who talked a lot and I wasn't sure they had both oars in the water most of the time.

"Would ten thousand dollars help?" the person asked innocently.

"Well, of course that would make a huge difference," I wistfully replied like a man remembering what he could do when he was twenty years younger.

"Well, I'll come by tomorrow and give you ten thousand dollars," was the matter-of-fact response.

I felt like patting the short little person on their crazy head while saying "There, there, . . . how nice," like I was patronizing a puppy.

We met the next day. The person came to the church, but I had quite forgotten the conversation. Just for humor's sake and to see what might happen if we hung out for a bit, because I had learned by then that Jesus sometimes moves in offline spontaneous ways, I went along, down to the bank. The teller didn't even bat an eye or look askance when asked to draw up a cashier's check for $10,000 made out to the church. I stood there in disbelief. The church board decided to hold the check and not use it for a while in case some family member appeared later demanding we return the funds because the person was indeed as crazy as I had initially suspected.

It turns out this person owns a lot of property and lives homeless due to other reasons besides a lack of money. It wasn't enough to put us totally over the top, but if God did something new it would make a ton of difference to buy us time to see if God had other plans unfold. We were going to hold the funds in reserve to give back if things didn't work out. Meanwhile we just kept on with our closing plans.

In our denomination, the local church owns all its assets and titles to property unless it closes down. If we closed, all the assets would revert to the denomination according to the bylaws. In January, we had a couple denominational leaders come and consult with us again. They advised us to close the church and perhaps come up with an alternative strategy to keep some kind of ministry to the poor going in the aftermath. I wrote just such a proposal and submitted it to the denomination when I went to our annual mid-winter conference in Chicago at the end of that month.

I came home, and our church leaders scheduled a congregational meeting for mid-February to lay on the table our plans to close by April. We knew it would take several months to clean out the place, conduct closing services, transfer or sell assets and generally lay this ministry appropriately in the grave. Hopefully to stay down this time.

The problem was — I didn't get any response from the denomination by the time of the congregational meeting, so we took care of other business and tabled our closure talks for one more month—until the end of March. I wasn't too panicky, because if we needed it the ten grand was still in the bank to be used in dire emergency and we could reimburse the donor upon sale of the building. I would feel awfully guilty taking such a sum and then closing down.

The first week of March, our Regional Conference Superintendent came out to meet with our Leadership Team. He confessed that even though we had been talking with them for some time about our situation, his heart broke when he read the proposal to close down. He then spent the month of February working behind the scenes with other denominational leaders on our behalf for an alternate solution.

Four factors were converging at this moment to change the story for us. First of all, our church *was* growing. When I came there were just over thirty people on a Sunday. More than half of them had left since, but a typical Sunday now saw around seventy people, not all of whom are sober (and definitely not clean), I admit, but they're still there to worship and meet God.

The second factor was that our ministry to the poor was too good to shut down and we hadn't quit. The superintendent confessed that no one thought we would still be going by now. Many people talked behind the scenes of us closing last summer, then in the fall, then in December. Both the local non-profits and our own denomination were stunned we were still standing, like Rocky at the end of the first movie. We were the long shot bet that no one would count on, but secretly hoped would win. I felt as beaten and battered as Rocky, but we still stood. The denomination had simply underestimated the stubbornness of my wife and I, when we get thrown into battle. The Biblical word for that is *perseverance,* but sometimes it's hard to tell the difference. Sometimes it's a really fine line between faithful and stupid.

The third factor was that the current business market meant the property value had plummeted. The site was worth over two million a few years before. Its worth had plummeted to only one point three million. The only written offer we had received after having the place on the market for six months was for half of that. One local church had with us to make a purchase offer but in the end their offer consisted of having us give them the site and they would let us stay for one more year feeding the downtown homeless. They would kindly pay me one-year wages for that. Since that would amount to them acquiring our property for less than ten percent of its value, we ungraciously declined.

The representative of the investment group for our denomination advised everyone that it would be better to keep the church afloat and have the building occupied for two or three more years by investing in it rather than take a substantial financial loss. In that neighborhood, if our church closed and was boarded up, it would become a homeless hotel, full of squatters (in less than thirty days). The Conference Office would hold title and deed to the property in Spokane, but they would be a five hour drive away in Seattle.

The fourth and final factor had to do with another church in our state closing down in Tacoma the previous year. A vacant building sitting in that city was a burden to the Conference. Our Executive Board didn't want to have another such a liability in Spokane. Timing is everything.

Instead of closing, it was proposed that we would receive an equity share loan on the building of up to $200,000 with payments of interest only for two to three years, to keep us going. In addition, the Conference would use some funds reserved for Eastern Washington ministry to help us install a new heating system. They also wanted to feature our church at the April Conference, meeting of churches from our four-state region, at which time they planned on taking an offering for our ministry to poor and feature us as a potential mission and work project site for other churches.

I didn't know it then, but that generous gift from a homeless person was buying us a few more months of life; without that, we would not have made it all. This was a major change. We knew we would there be around several more years. But there was still a long way to go.

We agreed to the loan and took the property off the market in March. But, the loan didn't fund in April. The Department of Church Growth and Evangelism wanted to get involved, making sure the deal was solid, saying that if we get such a loan numerous other churches will be lining up to ask for the same deal. They wanted a detailed plan explaining why we would get a "yes" to such a deal when other churches might get a "no." So, things were put on hold as I filled out detailed plans and budgets, and paperwork. The April deadline was pushed to June.

Because of the homeless person's $10,000 gift, we could stay financial alive past April, when we had projected to be flat broke. Thanks to that gift, the money we had would last until June. But somehow it stretched us into the end of August. There were a couple of strange circumstances that helped. The month of May saw a level of income that was high enough to not result in a loss for the first time in many, many years. We even got odd, unexpected money, like a refund from the IRS for overcharging us! One of our board members said they hadn't remembered a breakeven month in over a decade of their attendance. Don't ask me to explain the economics of how a church that lost thousands of dollars *every month* for over a decade was still standing. It doesn't make any sense.

The first phase of the loan, $60,000, came the last few days in July. We spent some to stay afloat each month and some to pay for much needed building projects. We knew we would need to borrow more to make it through 2012, but for a church that should have been dead—it was still quite amazing.

I, however, don't care for the stress and I wish God wouldn't do these things to me. He's making me old before my time. It's a fine line between faith and freak out, between steadfast and stubborn, between sure and stupid— I cross it a lot!

Isaiah 11:1-3 says, *"A shoot will come up from the stump of Jesse; from his roots a Branch will bear fruit. The Spirit of the LORD will rest on him— the Spirit of wisdom and of understanding, the Spirit of counsel and of might, the Spirit of the knowledge and fear of the LORD — and he will delight in the fear of the LORD". (NASB)*

This famous Christmastime verse is referring to the family line of King David (Jesse's son). Long after the life of this family line of kings and rulers had been cut down and forgotten, a man would be born in the family line, like a shoot coming up out of a stump everyone thought dead, to become even more glorious than King David ever was.

That inspired me at the end of that year. We know we are a small, humble church growing by desperately poor people. We aren't a great tree, just a little shoot. It seemed God had plans for us which were bigger than our own plans. My prayer going into 2012 was that God would bring us more joy, hope, and strength than we could imagine. That little bit of life extension we received in the equity loan, which we predicted would be two more years, would lead to something mighty, growing up out of dead stump.

SECTION 4: LIFE AMONG THE WALKING DEAD

Jonah's Prayer

Then Jonah prayed to the LORD his God from the stomach of the fish, and he said,
> 'I called out of my distress to the LORD,
> And He answered me.
> I cried for help from the depth of Sheol;
> You heard my voice.
> 'For You had cast me into the deep,
> Into the heart of the seas,
> And the current engulfed me.
> All Your breakers and billows passed over me.
> So I said, 'I have been expelled from Your sight.
> Nevertheless I will look again toward Your holy temple.'

Jonah 2:1-4 (NASB)

17. LIVING IN A PARALLEL UNIVERSE

I met with a couple of pastor friends from other downtown area churches. We meet regularly to talk and pray. One of them asked me, "So, how do the elderly like having the homeless in their church service?"

"Actually, they don't mind a bit," I answered. "Everyone knows that the only reason our denomination is willing to fund us and keep our ministry going is because of our work with the poor."

"So, in an odd twist," he laughingly answered, "those little old ladies have to be thankful that homeless alcoholics and addicts have saved their church!"

"Well, now that you put it that way—you're right," I mused. "I guess that would really only happen in some kind of odd, parallel universe," I joked; we both laughed.

I got to thinking about that funny insight and suddenly decided that I must be living in a parallel universe where the normal rules of social life no longer apply. Our board had come to the conclusion in December of 2010 that we couldn't financially survive past March 31, 2011. We made plans to begin the process of closing the church and dispersing come April of the same year. Early talks with denominational leaders had them advising us to close. I had submitted a plan for closure to them in early February. But, a homeless person who loves our church and its ministry gave us $10,000 to keep going. Only in a parallel universe would the financial answers to a church's crisis come from a homeless person. As a result, we could go to June.

In March, with the Superintendent's help, the denomination decided to help fund us instead. It was mostly due to our work with the poor and our signs of church growth. What church board meeting would decide that its answer to financial crisis and numerical decline would be to invite in homeless alcoholics and addicts? Not in our universe!

In my second year there, we had cleaned out the church six months after I first took over as the pastor and dumped sixty years' worth of accumulated stuff, totaling two and one-half tons!

I heard some of the many homeless people helping us comment, "Why can't they clean up after themselves? Why do these church people have to be so messy?" *Homeless drug addicts who camped under the freeway complained.* I thought that was another parallel universe moment!

I was getting musically and socially bored. I needed an outlet, a hobby to rejuvenate myself. The stress of the years of ministry and loneliness and isolation of this ministry had taken its toll on my health and body. I had high cholesterol and had to be put on high blood pressure medication due to stress. I had a special dental piece made to where at night because I ground and chipped my teeth at night while sleeping. I had nightmares every night for several years. Some kind of villain was always chasing me in my dreams and I had to kill them first. I didn't sleep much.

To reduce stress, I decided to return to one of my earliest loves of playing music and put together three hours' worth of performance music of Springsteen, Bob Seger, Van Morrison, old classic rocker tunes, some U2, and several modern country artists. I began playing at several wine bars around town just for fun. I found myself having some of the best evangelism moments I've had in years, inviting others to our church by singing in the wineries. *The Wine Bar helping our church to grow?* Not in my previous universe.

I met with a group of agency leaders who facilitate non-profit work among the poor. I attended a lot of these kinds of meetings since being involved with so many different groups working with the homeless. One of the ladies on the board with me was an extremely liberal-type who supports the aggressive antiwar, pro-marijuana work in Washington. Name an issue and she would fall on the extreme left of it. She also has connections with the gay community and is very proud of her atheistic, liberal position. She's, still, stunned that she is actually has a conservative pastor of an Evangelical Church as a friend. She insists on calling me *Pastor* Rob rather than just Rob, because she likes to blow her friends and family away with the knowledge that we're friends who work well together. Just to be shocking with them, she will begin a sentence with *"Pastor Rob says . . . "*

I had been invited to a symposium because she highly recommended me. I listened while she told the other members about her recent experiences. "You know how the underprivileged clients come into our offices very skeptical and cynical of the help we social workers offer?" She began as the group affirmed; "Well, all I have to do is ask them if they've been to First Covenant Church and when they say 'yes', I tell them that I'm friends with Pastor Rob and immediately all of their guard drops, and they trust me." She laughed.

It's in a parallel universe where a liberal, atheistic, social worker has to name-drop a conservative Christian to get in good graces with the poor. It must be in that same universe that the Christian and the social worker are genuine friends.

Peter addresses his first epistle to Christians who are "Strangers scattered throughout the world." He meant foreigners, aliens, and sojourners—those who don't really belong here but are only temporary visitors, whose home is elsewhere. If we're doing ministry right, shouldn't it be like we're from another universe?

In *Hebrews* (11:8, 10, *NASB*) the writer says this of Abraham: "By faith Abraham, when he was called, obeyed by going out to a place which he was to receive for an inheritance; and he went out, not knowing where he was going. By faith he lived as an alien in the land of promise, as in a foreign land, dwelling in tents with Isaac and Jacob, fellow heirs of the same promise; for he was looking for the city which has foundations, whose architect and builder is God."

And, in 11:16, the writer adds, "But as it is, they desire a better country, that is, a heavenly one. Therefore, God is not ashamed to be called their God; for He has prepared a city for them. *(NASB)*

I suppose if we belong to another reality, a heavenly realm, if our true dwelling is in God's house, then many of the rules and expectations of how the world actually works come from a parallel universe—a heavenly one. Living in a parallel universe should be the norm for all Christians. But it's still hard to get used to.

18. PLACEBO CHRISTIANITY AND A CLASH OF TEEN CULTURE

I found myself sitting in a coffee shop with a group of men once a week reading the book *Crazy Love* by Francis Chan (Publisher: David C. Cook, 2008) and discussing it. It's a great book by a former pastor of a mega-church in Southern California. In his writing, Chan wrestles with the assumptions and paradigms we have built in America about what church is, what it should be doing, and how people inside of it should operate. The premise is that if we were "crazy in love" with Jesus then we would act in ways that others would think are crazy—particularly when it came to helping the poor and needy.

I remember one section where he talked about buying a bag of groceries to give to a poor family and then driving around his neighborhood for hours because he honestly didn't know anyone who might need groceries. He had thousands of people who attended his church at the time. He didn't know anyone poor. What an indictment regarding the disconnect between the church and the poor.

One can read on Chan's Website that he is now bridging that gap: "In May 2010, he left Cornerstone to work directly in mission with the poor locally and internationally. He is also the Chancellor and Founder of Eternity Bible College and serves on the board of directors for Children's Hunger Fund, an international humanitarian aid foundation to assist the poor, and on the board for World Impact, an inner-city mission's organization dedicated to planting churches among the urban poor in America."

I thought it odd, as we read Chan's book and sipped our four-dollar coffees in a cozy North-side, trendy, artsy coffee house, how disconnected we all were. I watched while week after week, the dynamic and capable leader of the study tried to get the guys to engage and interact and "go deep" with each other—to no avail. We were just as removed as Chan was. Many of our guys talked about how they wish they could go on a mission trip someday or wish they could get more involved making a real difference against the forces of poverty, loneliness, hopelessness, and degradation. I invited them to come on down and help serve a meal and I would introduce them to some characters. No one took me up on the offer.

The funny thing was, I came to feel like we all thought we were growing in Christ and spiritual maturity because we were doing our small group Bible study thing. It felt like *placebo Christianity*, to me. A placebo is that little sugar pill that drug researchers give a test group telling them that it's actual medicine. They do this just to see if the psychological benefit of THINKING you are getting the real thing is as effective as the real thing itself.

That's when it hit me that I think we've created a Christian subculture where we believe that if we sit every week in a small group reading and discussing the latest book, it's the real thing in spiritual growth. So, *agreeing* with the book's ideas and premises became the important part—not *doing* them. It felt like a placebo.

James 1:22 says, "But prove yourselves doers of the word, and not merely hearers who delude themselves." *(NASB)*

After eight weeks or so, the study ended. I told the leader I was bowing out. I felt like too much of a maverick and I just don't seem to fit the Christian world anymore. I couldn't feel like I was growing simply because I joined a small group and I agreed with a book. Maybe I've just grown tired of deluding myself for so long. I couldn't help but contrast our placebo book study with the actions later shown by some teens.

On a Sunday some time afterward, a group of high school students (associated with a Young Life program) came down to our church to help cook and serve a meal to the homeless. The Young Life leaders were all former or current students at Whitworth University, dedicating their lives to making a difference in the youth culture around them. Usually, they gathered to build relationships, have some recreation, study the Bible, or talk about Christian ethics. This particular day they chose to add a service project for the poor to their schedule. They found us through a connection with another Young Life from Ione, a small town almost two hours' drive north. That small-town group had been coming down for over a year.

These new students were fantastic workers and were totally taken aback by how kind and thankful the homeless population turned out to be. Salvation Army had recently dropped off a bunch of blankets for us to distribute, so we put one brave young man to work, walking through the crowd and asking who needed a blanket. He beamed as he felt the pleasure of God while distributing the needed goods. Afterward he said that he felt both elated and troubled.

"It was great to be able to help, and I could tell they really appreciated it, but it also felt so small. Like a single blanket wasn't much compared with all the need they really had."

We agreed, but many times that's where it starts; the food and the blanket build trust, the trust builds confidence, which leads to an invitation to deeper talk, and many times that deeper talk leads us to Jesus.

The students and their leaders came out after serving the food and sat among the homeless, talking and sharing stories and learning what they could of life for those on the edges of society. The most touching moment came when two young runaway girls who are fellow students from a different high school, came through the line to get a meal. The two runaways had come to our meal last week for the first time and felt bold enough to attend church earlier that morning. They had been kicked out of the last church they tried to visit when they wandered over to the lost and found table and rummaged through the apparel left there. An usher booted them for that crime. It was a huge step for them to try church again.

One of them informed us that they wanted to keep coming to church. "I went to your prayer loft area during the service and asked God to come into me and take over," she said. "And you know what? I really felt Him! It was like He was right here with me and I could feel His warmth and love. I've never felt that ever before in my life!" She beamed.

We couldn't help but notice the contrast of youth culture. On one side of the counter stood high school students deeply loved by their families, living in secure homes, planning on going to college, active in after school activities, offering their service to others out of their affluence and privilege. On the other side are two high school runaways, neglected and abused by their families, fighting to stay in school, living in poverty and hunger, comforting their own pain with drugs, alcohol, or sex; all the while, they gratefully accepted the meal and scurried off into the gym to eat. *Both sets of teens* were heard, saying, "I felt God here today!"

19. JUST MAYBE

When I was in my freshman year of college at a Christian university, I experienced my first foot washing ceremony. It's one of those rituals that some Christians perform commemorating the Last Supper, where Jesus washed the Disciples' feet. In Jesus' time, that was the job of the lowliest slave. He was saying we should be willing to serve one another in humility, even being willing to do degrading, dirty, thankless tasks, for the sake of each other.

We sat on nice chairs in a lovely, lit chapel, while we each took off our shoes and socks and got our feet washed by the person on our left, then washed the feet of the person on our right. We sang songs and prayed prayers the whole time in a rather solemn ceremony. . . I hated it. The symbolism is lost in our culture. The one being ashamed was the person *getting* their feet washed, not *doing* the washing. It was the opposite in Jesus' time, so I thought it was a dumb, ritualistic ceremony about how to feel low, humble, and degraded for the sake of service *without actually doing anything real.*

I had a flashback memory of that ceremony in June. I don't know what it was. Maybe the bucket of water I held at the time, maybe it was the lighting of the sunset, or a just some sound unlatching a forgotten memory in my cerebral cortex. Maybe it was the Holy Spirit. I took the bucket of water and sloshed off a pile of vomit on the back-entrance steps of the church... no ceremony required. It was during a street evangelism event that we were doing in our parking lot.

The vomit belonged to Red Rob. He's an alcoholic homeless man who'd been coming to our meals for over a year. All summer he lived in the third juniper bush from the right on the eastside of our building. He is the one who apologized to me for breaking one of our faux stained-glass windows which we covered with a plywood board. He was the one who had been shoved into the glass during a fist fight. The fight happened when Red Rob was sitting on the stairs smoking a cigarette and watching that couple "get it on" (as I mentioned in my opening story).

"You gotta do something about him!" was the challenging cry his angry accuser hurled at me.

I had mumbled something about how the whole landscape was going to be torn out in a week or so and everyone would have to move off church property and conduct all their "business" somewhere else anyway. I was too tired to get into it. He doesn't have to worry about being watched anymore because a few days after the bushes were torn up Red Rob was found dead in a back alley by a couple of passers-by. They said he died of natural causes.

I often wondered what caused so much pain and hopelessness in Red Rob's life that in two years I never saw him sober. And I saw him several times a week, what with him living in the third bush from the right and all. I often wondered about his childhood. I mean, what new mom ever holds their baby to the breast thinking *he's going to grow up to be living in a bush as an addict and will die, cold, alone and friendless, to be found the next day by some passers-by?* Something in life had to really go wrong. Red Rob used to tell me how he went to an elementary school in Sandpoint, Idaho, and Sarah Palin was in his third-grade class. Wow, are those two different trajectories. What happened to that little boy?

I wonder ...does God care? ...Do we care? ...Do *you* care? I know God, because it's all over his Word, about how much he likes the poor, the lost, the lonely, the oppressed, the downtrodden, and the afflicted.

Here's an example from Isaiah, 58:5-7:

> *You humble yourselves by going through the motions of penance, bowing your heads like reeds bending in the wind. You dress in burlap and cover yourselves with ashes. Is this what you call fasting? Do you really think this will please the*

Lord? *"No, this is the kind of fasting I want: Free those who are wrongly imprisoned; lighten the burden of those who work for you. Let the oppressed go free, and remove the chains that bind people. Share your food with the hungry, and give shelter to the homeless. Give clothes to those who need them, and do not hide from relatives who need your help. (New Living Translation, NLT)*

I wonder if Red Rob was sent to our church in the last year and a half of his life as a final chance, as a last-ditch effort on God's part to put him in the path of people who carry a message of hope, healing, and salvation for a guy living in the third bush from the right. Maybe. . . . . . Maybe.

I wonder what might have happened if more of us Christians who attend this church would have joined these guys at our church sponsored lunch each week. Would there have been enough of us present that someone would have said something instrumental to Red Rob by befriending him? . . . . . Maybe.

I wonder if all summer long, there were more than just two of us from the church eating in a room with one hundred and fifty of these folks, someone might have had the chance to meet him and share the love of Jesus with him. Or If there were more people willing to serve in the kitchen then the three to four faithful workers who are always there could've been freed up to come out and mix with the homeless and someone could've offered a prayer of healing and salvation, powerful enough to have changed Red Rob's destiny. Then he might not have died alone and friendless in a back alley. Maybe... Maybe.

Maybe if some of the many people who've visited our meals from other large churches would have actually kept coming back like they said there were going to do, one of them might have been there to be used by Jesus for the sake of Red Rob. I hear a lot about how young people today want to attend churches that are on the cutting edge of works projects, doing ministry with the poor. Maybe if three or four of the two dozen Christian University students who have visited our church over the last two years would've stayed and worked with us, instead of leaving to join the cool big church with the hip, shaved-headed pastor and the rocking band where all the all the students attend, then maybe things would've been different for Red Rob because that *one* student would've saved his life. Maybe... Maybe.

Maybe, if just one of the elderly people who continue to come to church every week and sit in the same spot on the same pew like they have for years and decades, listening to sermons and reading the Bible, singing all those hymns of Christian inspiration, and storing up godly wisdom two to three times longer than many of the rest of us have been alive would've gotten up to befriend the guy living in the third bush from the right, just outside the window, the wanderer might not have died alone and friendless in a back alley, a block or two away from their church. Maybe... Maybe.

I know our Sunday afternoon meals are terribly inconvenient. I've been told so by other pastors and Christians. They tell me that the Sunday afternoon time slot is just "bad" for them and if we would move it to another day and time they might come and help. I hoped that even giving up one Sunday afternoon a month might be a reachable goal, but I've discovered that it's just an inconvenient time even for that much. But since Sunday is the only day no else for many, many city blocks are serving a meal, we kind of feel like the hunger of the poor is the determining factor of when we should serve the meal and not how convenient it is for our activity schedule. I know it's *very* inconvenient. Believe me! Especially when I can only get a small number of people to help in the kitchen and it's just two of us out in the room to share Jesus and sometimes we aren't very good at it. I'm terribly sorry and I whole heartedly agree that it is darn inconvenient.

Maybe if I was just a way better pastor I could share some insight and knowledge from God's word to inspire and teach us, find something to help us all with this predicament. But, it's a funny thing, you can read every single one of the thousands of words in the Bible and all the hundreds and hundreds of pages and you won't find the word *inconvenient*, not anywhere, not even using several different English translations. So, I'm stuck with how to help and give counsel about our problem here. I can find words like *hardship, affliction, pain, suffering, persecution*, and *perseverance*, but nothing on *inconvenience*. I even found some phrases that kind of relate about "dying to ourselves," "picking up our cross," "crucifying our fleshly desires," "enduring the race before us," and others, but these seem too extreme to help us when dealing with situations that are inconvenient.

It's such a powerful word for us. This, opposition to *convenience*, stops us from doing things; it directs our choices, determines our activities, and generally has as much force on our lives as the power of gravity. We do or don't do tons and tons of things based on how convenient they are. But unfortunately for us, even though the word is one of our most useful and powerful words, it's not in God's vocabulary at all. I just have no counsel to offer us from His word on this matter.

I hope if God sends one more person to spend the last months of his life close by us like Red Rob (a guy He already knows is destined to die alone and friendless in a nearby back alley, only to be discovered by some passers-by in the morning) that God will understand our confusion on what to do since we don't use the same vocabulary as He does. We hope He won't judge us too harshly. Maybe... Just Maybe.

After publishing this newsletter article, I heard from several homeless people that Red Rob picked the Juniper bush at our building to set up his home because – we were one of the only places he felt any kind of affection. We knew him by name and we were always kind to him.

---

20. THE POWER OF SMALL THINGS

One day, a young woman came up to me during the homeless meal and handed me a card. It was a hand written thank you note, for all we have done for her and her boyfriend. She had been coming to our meals for almost two years. Her street name is Sunshine. I had to kick her out once, for going off on another lady during Gonzaga's Thursday night meal, when she almost got into a brawl. She came back the next week apologizing for her mouth and behavior; she'd been cool since. A lot of these people need more than a second chance.

"I just can't thank you enough for all you have done for me," she gushed.

"What do you mean?" I responded, since I couldn't really remember doing anything particularly grand for her.

"Last winter, me and my boyfriend got into our own apartment for the first time in a long time – you gave us those sheets of plastic?" she answered in a tone trying to helpfully remind me how I had been such a crucial part of her year.

We keep rolls of painter's plastic on hand so that whenever it rains, guys and ladies camping out can cut off a good ten or twelve-foot section and cover their camp spot or lay it on the ground to keep them dry. Sunshine and her boyfriend were given several yards of plastic last winter after they had moved into their apartment.

"We used that plastic to cover our windows and our heat bill dropped from $145 a month to $80 a month," she excitedly said, adding with a sigh of relief, "That was the difference between us being able to eat or pay the phone bill or sometimes getting a bus pass each month. It literally saved us. We were so broke before that, we fell behind in rent and thank God, the landlord was kind to us and let us stay anyway. With that extra amount, we could get caught up and back on our feet."

"I thought your housing was subsidized?" I responded, "Doesn't that kind of guarantee that you're able to stay?"

"Not really. You see, I have to support my three kids and my boyfriend has one child to support with his check."

I had never seen them with children, so I asked, "Where are your kids?"

"They're in the foster care system and one is with my mom. Most of our government paychecks have child support taken out so there really isn't near as much to live on for us," she explained. "I don't mind, though; I'm glad I can help them. Without your meals every Sunday and Gonzaga's every Thursday night, along with the dog food for our pet you give us each week, we wouldn't have made it."

Leaning in close she added, "You know I used to be a hardcore meth addict and heroin user. I've been clean for almost 11 years now. Without you guys helping us, I know that I would've gone back to using again, because I wouldn't have been able to take the stress anymore. I almost didn't make it as it was—*but I did! Thank you so much!*"

She then told me how she had been praying to God more than ever before in her whole life and she felt like He wanted her to start giving back somehow. At the homeless shelter, House of Charity, a block away from our church, there is a Hispanic man who is a janitor. She said she always sees him with a smile on his face and a positive attitude, even when he is cleaning up feces that were spread all over sinks and mirrors by some psycho nutjob at the shelter. He always smiles and stays positive. She was thinking about giving back when she saw him one day leaving a church service somewhere. He had his seven kids in tow. Sunshine felt God say to her – "NOW, HIM!" So, she gave him fifty bucks that she had saved. That was a ton of money to her. She was beaming at me when she told me how she felt when giving it away because God told her to do it.

"It felt great," she exclaimed!

The card she was handing me had a hand drawn picture on the inside of a sun peaking over the horizon with a smiley face drawn on it and rays of light shooting off into the heavens. The note read: "Thanks. Can't express our thankfulness for the support you've shown us. Knowing you guys is a great blessing. It was the good of others not giving up on us that gave us the strength we so need. Thank you for setting a good example, for that is the true teachings of God!"

I couldn't help but think of, Mark, 12:41-44, "Jesus sat down near the collection box in the Temple and watched as the crowds dropped in their money. Many rich people put in large amounts. Then a poor widow came and dropped in two small coins. Jesus called his disciples to him and said, "I tell you the truth, this poor widow has given more than all the others who are making contributions. For they gave a tiny part of their surplus, but she, poor as she is, has given everything she had to live on." New International Version (NIV)

"Painter's plastic and dog food saved her life and kept her off drugs," I thought. WOW! Who would've guessed?! Sometimes, it's the small things.

One day a guy we called Cowboy Mike came shuffling into church in the timidest manner I'd ever seen him. Cowboy Mike was around sixty and had been a dentist in his former life. I guess he went through a bitter divorce and the wife took most of everything. In the end, he found himself working for her alimony and to keep the business going. I don't know if he started drinking before or after that, but in the end, he just walked away from it all and became a homeless vagabond. He had enough money in the bank that he could periodically fly himself to places like Texas and enter rodeos as a bull rider. I think he had a not-so-secret death wish. He would brag that he was always the oldest bull rider at every rodeo he entered. He was a man's man. Walking in timid was not his usual style.

With his head down and glancing up in quick, furtive looks he waved me over to him in quick motions. "I hope it's okay," he whispered to me, "but I had to tell you in advance that I had to have a couple of beers today to work up the courage to come to church. Is that okay?"

On the inside, I felt like saying, "I know the feeling," but instead, I asked, "Are you gonna be okay? You'll be well behaved today?"

"Oh yeah," he assured me, "I'll be good." With that, he shuffled up front to the second row and sat all through church with a look of wondrous awe. Afterward, he told me it was the first time in thirty years he'd been to a church service. He was misty-eyed as he promised to keep coming back. He came for a while and a few weeks later I never saw or heard from him again. I asked around, but no one knew whatever happened to Cowboy Mike. I heard someone say they thought he got a job washing dishes at the local men's shelter last time they saw him. Maybe the rodeo finally got him. I like to think that the small things we did with dinner and conversation, and those few church services, had an impact on his life and his choices.

One of the hardest things about downtown urban ministry is that the small tasks completed often add up and help move people toward a changed life. When that happens, one of the first things they do is get out of downtown and the old life. Never seeing someone again can either mean we were very successful or that we lost one. We often never know which it really is. All we have left are the small things we did or said that mattered in the right moment, and the trust that Jesus has people in his care, not ours.

21. THE NATURE OF PREACHING

On Christmas Day, a homeless couple came into church that had been coming to our meals for over a year. They had never been to a church service before. I had taken time over the previous weeks to go out of my way to invite them, assuring them that they would be welcome and would like our service.

They got up early, packed up their campsite and hiked over to church. We had made special handout gift bags for our homeless friends who attended service that day. Socks, gloves, tooth paste, military MREs (hot meals ready to eat in a bag), candy bars, and some reading material. They loved the service.

Afterward, I spoke with the man, who is a friend of mine. We've had many a great conversation over the last several months. He was obviously deeply touched by something that happened in the service. I asked him why he didn't come more often, because he was always welcome here.

His eyes misted over as he started to reply. His lower jaw trembled, and with the first syllable he spoke, his voice cracked. He had to stop to gather himself as he held back tears. He tried and failed at a couple more attempts to speak. After a moment with deep sadness in his eyes he choked out, "I can't. I cry too much in church." With that, he turned and walked away to avoid breaking down.

Every three months, or so, he comes in beaten and battered,

with a black and blue face. He is, generally, a mean drunk; he drinks a lot. He's tried to sober up many times in the last year. Once, when he was tapering off his drinking to just one beer a day, he would excitedly report to me a couple of times a week about his progress. He got the shakes so bad during that time he couldn't put on a pair of socks. He would come early to set up tables and stay after our meals to help clean up the place. He needed to stay busy.

"I cry too much in church". Those words spoke so much about lost hopes and lost dreams. Whoever aspires to being a homeless man when they grow up? When he sits in church he remembers what life was supposed to be. He thinks of all the choices, the pains, and wounds of the accumulated years. He thinks of all of the *should-have-beens* and the *could-have-beens*, all of the *if-onlys*; all the lost chances, broken relationships, and the evil he has done, and which has been done to him.

Does God still love me? Is His power big enough to reach even the depths of my life? How did I end up like this? Is there ever going to be a way out? Does anyone sitting around me think I'm worth rescuing? — "I cry too much in church."

He is around fifty years-old now. He thinks it's too late for him and that he will die alone in the street someday. He feels like he is on a runaway train and the tracks are washed out ahead. It's just a matter of *when* — not *how*. He believes that there is no other true destiny for him. He's tried and failed too many times to hope any longer.

"I cry too much in church." Those are the words of a heart that is still alive. Those are words coming from the depths of a soul that can still see clearly and can assess the situation with truth. Those words indicate that when he comes into the presence of the Holy Spirit and can no longer drown out the voice of God with booze and brawling, something tender in him awakens. These words are from someone that still remembers the hopes and dreams and desires that a shipwrecked life still hold — way down deep. Words that say the child of God in that broken, battered and abused life is still in there; Locked and trapped in a prison of despair.

"The Spirit of the Lord is upon Me, because He has anointed Me to preach the gospel to the poor; He has sent Me to heal the brokenhearted, to proclaim liberty to the captives and recovery of sight to the blind, to set at liberty those who are oppressed;" Jesus says in *Luke,* 4:18. How? What's the plan? How does this man experience that Jesus?

"How, then, can they call on the one they have not believed in? And how can they believe in the one of whom they have not heard? And how can they hear without someone preaching to them?" *(Romans,* 10:15)

Preaching! That's something a professional does from a platform in front of a gathered crowd—right? Not in *this* neighborhood. Oh, that happens too but something deeper is needed to reach a black and blue heart that cries too much in church.

A group of volunteers came down to serve at one of our meals and we spoke about reaching the deeply oppressed. "These guys aren't going to jump because some hotshot speaker rallies them with a nice speech," I said. "Their only hope to find the real Jesus is if a Christian picks a few of them to befriend, and walks with them for many months through the conflicts of life. Someone has to take time to hear their stories, follow up with them weekly, advise, counsel, and train them in the ways of God. One gifted speaker here won't make much of an impact. But twenty Christians willing to be real friends could." I often wonder where we can find those twenty Christians.

The ancient words of Jesus of Nazareth are still true — *The harvest is ripe, but the laborers are few.*

22. ETHICAL DILEMMAS

A young couple came to our meal once and asked us for help. She had just lost a baby in her fifth month of pregnancy. She said the shelter she stayed in had her climbing up into the top bunks because she wasn't high enough on the priority sign-up sheet to get a lower bed. She said she felt something "pop" inside her climbing into the bunk and not long after, she found herself in the bathroom holding a tiny baby in her hands until it died.

On a typical day, the shelter kicks everyone out with their stuff at 8:00am, so she left that morning like all the others, dragging her suitcases behind her walking the streets, drifting to other day shelters, and wandering downtown with her boyfriend.

No, they weren't married – Almost all the couples never are down here. Her health was poor, her nutrition was substandard, her lifestyle – let's just say it was incredibly twisted for someone wanting to bring a happy, healthy baby into the world. Her parenting and social skills were never developed in the family she grew up in. her only examples in that arena are *of what not to do.*

For the next few days the other women in the shelter scolded her and blamed her for losing the baby and not taking care of herself, telling her she killed that child with her own stupidity. One or two were kind and compassionate and expressed sorrow to her.

In a daze and in pain she and her boyfriend wandered the streets for a couple more days until Sunday came and they thought maybe they would give church and God a chance to move in their lives and see if He still cared about them at all. That Sunday morning, they decided to drift to a church service for the first time ever, though not ours.

I understood that he had a church background as a kid but when his mother tragically died ten years before he left the church and never returned staying angry at God the whole time. After the service, they worked up the courage to go to the pastor and ask if the church would help them get a hotel room, so she could physically recover and get away from the other shelter women. The church said no, because they weren't married, and it would be a sin and they didn't want to contribute God's money to help people sin. The guy offered not to stay with her but go back to his shelter each night, but since there wasn't any way to verify this, the church still said no. They then wandered the several blocks down to our meal on that Sunday afternoon and asked us if we would help them get a stay in a hotel room to recover.

What would you say? What would you do? What would you have suggested be done? For the record that other church wasn't wrong. I know that pastor and he is a good guy. He has been downtown longer than I and he even gets up extra early each and every Sunday and takes a guitar down under the freeway and conducts a church service for the homeless, often giving away breakfast treats and gloves and hats. He does this before his own church service starts and he does it rain or shine – even when it snows. They are familiar with the street population too and know that half the stories we hear are lying, con-games. Helping an unmarried couple have a hotel room for a couple of nights is not standard Christian or Biblical practice. Most churches I've attended would've also negated such a proposition.

I wasn't at the meal that day so some of our other leaders had to wrestle with the ethical dilemma of how to help, if at all. They verified the story through some of our street friends. They decided that after losing a baby so soon, fornicating probably wasn't going to be high on the woman's list of activities. Going strictly off compassion, they decided to get her a hotel room to recover in. Do you think that was wrong?

Ten years of raging at God, hating His standards for life, living opposed to His moral codes, in rebellion to His word and His ways, defiant against His Spirit, in a moment of tragedy they ask God for a touch of compassion through the church.

Did they deserve anything from His hand? Decidedly no! Were they complete and total sinners inside and out? – Oh yes. There is much more to their story than I am telling here. It's very dark, ugly, and filled with pain and destruction. Was this going to be the moment of change and transformation for them? Only God knew. Would opening that door of transformation by grace through an act of compassion be a good move? We thought, yes. What if we were wrong and they simply took advantage of the moment and went back to the way things always had been? – That was a risk for sure. Who was taking that risk? We thought maybe God was. Would God hold us accountable? Probably, but for which action, turning them away or getting the room?

The problem we face is that we believe in the grace of God, but we really like it when there is some incredible change first on the part of the sinner who demonstrates that they appreciate the grace, are thankful to God for it, and demonstrate through their behavior that they do in fact deserve a touch of grace. But by its very definition that then ceases to be grace and instead becomes an act of merit. Grace is really tough at the point of contact.

But I, for one, am thankful that when I have been raging at God, hating His standards for life, living opposed to His moral codes, in rebellion to His word and His ways, defiant against His Spirit and, in my moments of tragedy and brokenness, ask God for a touch of compassion and grace – He still gives it. *That's* the Gospel. That is why it's called *Good News*.

23. FOR EMERGENCY, TRY SERVICE

On a warm Monday night, we walked out of a church board meeting to discover a homeless man passed out cold on the loading dock by the back door. One of our board members discovered him initially and, after trying unsuccessfully to revive the man, came and got me. I recognized him right away even though he was lying face down in a puddle of his own drool.

I've seen this guy get sober at least twice in the last couple of years, attempting to change his life around. But the allure of the street and the swampy quicksand of downtown decadence out here pull broken people back under, time after time. This guy can play piano beautifully. I've told him if he ever gets thirty days of sobriety under this belt I would love to have him come play piano before services as our guests come in.

But this day he was in the worst shape I had ever seen him. I called his name and shook him forcefully trying to wake him, but nothing worked.

"Call 9-1-1" I instructed my board member.

As someone dialed, I continued to try and roust the guy. Finally, with his face plastered to the sidewalk in the pool of drool and his eyes still shut tight he mumbled, "Schling flob muh."

I was already on my hands and knees, so I leaned over real close to his face and gently spoke his name asking, "What? What did you say?"

"Sching fo meh," he repeated slightly more understandable.

"You want me to sing for you?" I asked incredulously.

"Ya," was all he could say still face down with his eyes shut tight and his body unmoving.

Not exactly knowing what else to do I put a hand on his shoulder and one on his back and began slowly and resonantly singing over him — "*Amazing grace, how sweet the sound* ...his eyes snapped open... *That saved a wretch like me...*" He began to stir trying to lift himself up... "*I once was lost but now I am found, was blind but now I see...*" By then, he had pulled himself up on his elbows, rolled over, wiped his face with his sleeve and was trying to sit against the building.

I kept singing— "*'twas grace that taught my heart to fear and grace my fears relieved...*" By the end of the second verse he could stand on his feet. He was singing with me now and trying to raise his hands up in worship. We ended our third verse together about being in Heaven ten-thousand years. He was on his feet but very wobbly.

"We've called 9-1-1 and they are on their way. I think you should sit awhile until they get here. Hey, I've got to ask, why are you here?"

"I knew if I could make it to the church I would be okay. I knew God would be here and He would look out for me," he responded in much less slurred fashion than he mustered only moments before. He was trying to get up close to the church building, like crawling under the umbrella of God while in a broken, weak, and hopeless state, before life rained down on him once more.

The fire trucks arrived, and the paramedics were mad at us that they came out for nothing but a drunk. Our guy refused care and wouldn't be taken to detox. There wasn't much anyone could legally do for him after that. The fire truck packed up and went back to their "real work" at the fire station, giving us disgusted and mean looks and we sat our man down to try to talk with him.

He requested I pray for him, so I did; but in his inebriated state, I don't think it took much hold. He was bobbing and weaving too much like a punched-up boxer in the fifteenth round, so my prayers couldn't land a good blow to his head. I finally convinced him he couldn't just stay here and sleep on the doorstep of the church since it wasn't safe for him. I watched him stagger and stumble off into the sunset heading to the homeless shelter two blocks away. It hardly felt like a victorious moment.

I stood there awhile on the loading dock wondering if all our work, prayer, conversations, meals and time really meant much. I asked God, "Are we really doing anything here at all that is worthwhile?" And I thought to myself, "This moment seems so petty and miniscule; in the grand scheme of the Kingdom of God, are we wasting our time?"

Jesus asked me to reflect a bit before going inside "What do you see here? What do you know about what you see?" He asked.

I know that when people are drunk the studies show that they know what's right and wrong and they know what they're doing morally – they just don't care. I also know people become alcoholics to numb pain they no longer know how to deal with. Many can't even name the pain any longer. I know the addiction is a powerful force, physically and psychologically. More powerful than a mere individual can fight by will power alone.

So, this guy, whom I've never seen in this bad a shape was numbing his great pain with total inebriation. When all his psychological and physical defenses were down, he crawled to the church as the one place where he believed he could find safety and security. He was crawling to the one place where he might find a touch of grace and get close enough to God to find protection and hope; the prodigal son trying to get home to the father.

He has never attended a church service, to my knowledge. If he has, it's only been one or two where he could hide in the very back lobby watching the service through the glassless windows like a man in the court of the Gentiles, "too unclean" to come into the temple.

He felt God's love here, not because of great preaching or dynamic worship music or creative brochures. He felt God's love in this place because almost every week somebody takes time to cook him a meal and serve it without judgment or condescending expectations. To this man, God's love was evident because people serve. Our mission to the poor is called Street Wise. Its slogan, borrowed from an old book by Dr. Joe Aldrich titled, *Gentle Persuasion* (1988; Publisher, Multnomah) is: "Love them until they ask why." He already knew why. It's because of Jesus.

The Holy Spirit reminded me: "His story isn't over yet, and you don't know the importance of this moment in this chapter of his life." In the end, he doesn't stand before me or any other person. He must give an account of his life to God the Father Almighty. And on that day, he will stand alone. On that day, I trust God will point us out as one, among the many times in his life when he was given a chance to see and accept the light of life.

If you serve others and if worry that you don't speak enough about Christ, just keep on loving them until they ask the reason, and wait for your chance. *Some already know the answer!*

24. A TRAILER-LOAD OF GRACE

"Well, they've called me out as a bluffer," I thought to myself while I hooked up my flatbed trailer one Monday morning, on a cold day in February. "What else is there to do now, but to prove I'm not kidding by hauling all their junk to the dump?" I felt a little gleeful and excited at that last part.

On the Friday before, the Spokane Police had pushed out everyone who had been living under the freeway, two blocks from the church. Many of them had packed up their tent-city structure, loaded their shopping carts, and just wandered off. It was just too bad that several of them simply moved their entire camp to our parking lot and in front of one of our main entry doors.

We told them on Friday night that they couldn't stay and would have to move on. We said it again on Saturday – and again Sunday morning as we arrived at church. Only, on Sunday morning some punk, dope-addict kid decided to be all foul-mouthed and nasty to me. I'm pretty low tolerant of that kind of thing anymore – so I happily "got all up in his business," as they say.

It's at times like these I think of the Holy Scriptures; Proverbs, 10:14 "Wise men store up knowledge, but the mouth of a fool invites ruin." Or Proverbs, 14:3, "A fool's talk brings a rod to his back," and Proverbs, 18:6, "A fool's lips bring him strife, and his mouth invites a beating." Yes, one day I shall have to start a newsletter article with the words, "Pastor Rob was found fulfilling the Scriptures last week in an alley between 2nd and 3rd Avenue."

I know you're probably shocked and think we should be all lovey-dovey on the poor, wretched, downcast, folks but that's because you may not have spent enough time with them. Once, my friend, Mike, decided to spell me for an afternoon and take over watching and guarding the main dining room from trouble. He likes to talk about being full of love and he always posts things on Facebook and Twitter about helping those less fortunate. But that day, he went home cussing like a sailor from helping the poor.

It happens, now and then, that someone has to stand on the frontline and intercept trouble, so that everyone else, volunteering, can have fun. Usually, that's me – that day it was Mike. It all started for him when a crazy lady asked if he was Adolf Hitler's lover; things kind of went downhill from there... but I digress.

I gleefully hooked up the trailer and headed down to the church on that crisp Monday morning. The day before, I had called the cops to have them move the camp along – three times. Once that morning, once around 1:00 pm (when they showed up to simply inform them to leave) and then again around 5:00 pm as I was leaving and saw that nothing was happening.

The lady on the non-emergency cop line was rather annoyed with me and told me the police were too busy handling real problems. She told us we were totally free to haul any junk from our private property to the dump. Since the offending party wouldn't take instruction from us, nor would the cops do anything, what was left but to go down to the men's shelter and recruit some of my bigger, meaner homeless friends to help me haul the camper's junk to the dump in exchange for a Big Mac? I was honestly looking forward to an altercation with mouthy-Proverbs-boy.

When I arrived at church about one third of the mountain of junk was moved. A few homeless guys who help us clean the church had already taken action and hauled the humongous pile next to the cyclone fence along the vacant lot across the alley. I pulled into the parking lot with equal parts disappointment and relief. The owners of the pile were nowhere to be seen. I had just stepped inside and was talking to the guys who had moved the pile when a knock came at the door.

"Who owns the truck with the trailer attached?" A middle-aged woman on crutches asked hopefully. "Oh please, oh please, could you help me move my things? I finally got an apartment but it's about twenty blocks from here and I have no way to move my things and haven't since the police gave notice to kick us out from under the freeway. About half the stuff belongs to my roommate but she's in jail right now and can't help me."

She went to use the restroom while we stood around discussing her request for help. We all knew her; her street name was Mardi Gras. No one knew her real name. She was unusually ornery, even for a street person.

"I'm not gonna help her – ever." One guy exclaimed with finality. He knew her and couldn't stand her. "She's a mouthy, belligerent drug addict and I've had enough run-ins with her that I wouldn't help her ever with anything," and he left.

The other three guys and I discussed, "What would Jesus do?" This is the part of the story where I should also mention that she pulled a knife once on a board member during a meal when he was trying to get her to behave properly over some issue or another. He was experienced enough to calm her down and get her out. Would Jesus help an ungrateful and unthankful person whose behavior simply didn't deserve any kindness at all?

Why yes, He would. That's the heart of the message of grace. All of us have been unthankful, ungrateful, and belligerent. We are all undeserving wretches who weren't owed an ounce of kindness, yet a loving God showed us every kindness under Heaven, anyway. This is what it means to love like Jesus loved. I only have my trailer down here about three times a year. What were the odds I would have it that day to "help" her? I felt like Jesus had set me up.

So, a guy named Mouse who lives under the Maple Street Bridge, Phil our new custodian who used to be a drug dealer, and John, who was just drunk enough to wobble and slur his words (but not so drunk he couldn't help), joined me in loading her stuff on my trailer and moving her to her new apartment across town. I could sense Jesus smiling at me the whole time.

"And *you* thought you were hooking up the trailer to haul her stuff to the dump today," Jesus laughed continuously, "All the while I was planning on using you to help her out."

That's His grace; kindness to those of us who don't deserve it.

25. SCATTERING SEED

I was speaking with a friend once who often came down to our facility almost every Friday night to work with Union Gospel Mission's outreach team. They had been coming down for three years providing what amounts to the only Friday night meal in the neighborhood for the poor. They came because they can relax the Union Gospel Mission rules here. Guys didn't have to pass a Breathalyzer; they didn't have to behave in the strict codes the mission holds; the mission staff and personnel can dispel rumors and myths about their work, and they can use personal invitation to get more guys who are living on the edge to come to the mission's program. We benefitted because the mission paid us $250 a month for the privilege of using our gym.

This guy and I were talking about spiritual expectations, change, and growth in the people we work with. "Sometimes ya really are just scattering seed," he sighed with a note of resignation.

I knew what he meant. All of us who work among the poor and destitute walking dead of society know what he meant.

You can't go to church for long and not heard the Parable of the Soils from Jesus, in Mathew, 13, Mark, 4, or Luke, 8. The Parable of the Soils is how I've heard that described my whole life. Some call it The Parable of the Sower but, no matter, every sermon, blog or article you read on it talks about the soils and how each reacts to the seed, which is the word of God. The focus is on being the right kind of soil, having the right heart to hear God.

The truth is we modern people think that's dumb farming. Good farmers spend millions on machinery and land to cultivate the ground, fertilize it, treat it, and plow trenches and rows to plant in. Farmers get university degrees in engineering and have specialists who consult and train them on the use of equipment, the kinds of seed used, and the weather patterns of the area. Good farmers today have to be highly educated and technological wizards. They are experts in soil erosion patterns and chemical compositions. They even study the stock market and have specialized software to track the growth, harvest, and right selling opportunities of their produce. They don't just go out and toss seed to the wind hoping for the best.

In church, we are taught the same thing. Good churches create intelligent, sustainable programs that create a path for people to follow in order to develop their spirituality. We invest in the right kinds of equipment and build the right kinds of spaces to enhance and draw the crowds in order to plant the seeds of our words in the proper ground. We have cultivated the environment, we have built the programs, and we have trained the specialists who are experts with children, youth, or adult small groups.

We watch and study the patterns of social, political, psychological, and economic issues so we know which seed to use in our sermon series. We fertilize the ground with our highly advanced technological music, arts, audio visual equipment, and printed brochures. We don't just willy-nilly toss up spiritual thoughts and truths hoping it lands in the right place.

And yet, as my friend sighed, I joined with him in staring down at my shoes, giving my heavy sigh of agreement. When I did suburban church, modern techniques worked really well, and it was easier to measure.

Downtown in poverty culture, it feels like we're just scattering seed. We set a meal and draw the poor and broken, the pawns and the outcasts, the suppressed and the oppressed; the disenfranchised and the marginalized, the least and the lost, the tossed out, turned out and tired out multitudes who have given up most hope.

They don't focus, they don't appreciate, and they don't pay close attention. We don't have the high-tech equipment, we don't have the great trappings, and we can't afford to hire the specialists. We're too few in number to push back in any significant way against the crush of human misery that walks in. We're too spread thin to focus diligently and carefully on our work to become experts. We use what we have at hand and often it isn't much. We are underequipped, undermanned, overstretched and overwhelmed.

Sometimes, the best tool we have is nothing more than a conversation. We try to share a thought about God or the Bible's view of life. We plant ideas and thoughts about deep spiritual ideas and concepts to people whom sometimes we don't know for sure are sane. We attempt to raise hope by demonstrating the love of God in tangible ways to people who don't act like they appreciate it. We try to inspire people who no longer believe in the future.

Sometimes, it feels like we're taking what resources we have and we're tossing it up in the air hoping for the best—scattering seed. I think the parable Jesus told is about the sower after all and not just about the soil. We keep scattering seed while we feel small, helpless, insignificant and foolish. We are trusting that Jesus really meant what he said. Some of that soil is really good and the growth belongs to God.

Our task is to be faithful in making sure that in our moment we honored Him with our lips and our actions. We speak his truth in meager handfuls; it's in a kind word, a smile of encouragement, a pair of shoes, a hug, a scripture promise, a prayer with a touch, a compliment inspiring their self-worth. Usually we have no idea the work that is being done in another's heart. We sow God's love and God's truth because somehow, somewhere in ways we won't see at first – it is taking root. A heart is changing, a mind is transforming, a life is growing - because we scattered and a single seed in a single moment, took root – and we trust in faith, will one day increase, one hundred times the investment.

26. JUST WHEN I'D HAD ENOUGH

"That's it! I'm done helping those two – I won't do anything for them again." That's what I told myself about a month ago after trying to assist two homeless people who have been coming here for meals and church off and on for three years. Tonia and I had tried to assist them from getting evicted, but it was not to be avoided. We helped them move their stuff to storage and then they missed several appointments and follow up visits with me over a period of two weeks. I spent time talking with lawyers and landlords, we even raised a little bit of money to re-establish them in an apartment again. But, after watching them totally disrespect themselves and us, I decided not to pass the help along. One missed appointment they came in so tweaked-out high that she couldn't stand up straight.

"I'm done helping two junkies, who don't care about their own lives," I vowed to myself. "I will spend my time and energies on people who are worthwhile. These two are a hopeless case," I thought to myself and decided to move on.

About that same time, I got a random sales call from a woman who helps churches raise funds by selling discount cards which provide special deals at local businesses. I described to her what our church was like and that fund raising was a desperate need for us but the crew to pull it off wasn't in our midst at present. A couple of days later she called me back and said she had been praying for us. She told me she had spent several years of her life as a homeless addict and some church in Texas kept coming downtown to her every week showing love. She said it took two years, but she finally trusted them enough to tell her story and she gave her life to Jesus. Now she works in a Christian company helping all kinds of churches all over the country raise money for youth groups and mission trips.

"Don't give up doing what you're doing" she told me. "You have no idea the impact you're having on people like me".

Dotty had come to our very first meal three years ago. "When you were passing out flyers to come and have a free meal at this church I couldn't believe it," she said to me when we first met;

"I've been homeless down here for years and this church never does nuthin' for nobody," she pronounced emphatically.

"Well I'm here now and we're going to try and change all that" I responded. Three years later and we were still trying.

Over the last several years we had helped Ronnie and Dotty many times with coats, blankets, food, advice, and help of any and all kinds. I've prayed *with* them and *for* them often. Many times, I've wondered to myself if we ever were really making a difference in their lives because it seems like drugs offered them far more of an answer, far more often. No matter what we did the life of the street always seemed to have way more power over them than our efforts.

About three weeks after giving up on them, I preached a sermon on the grace of Jesus Christ. It was about how our salvation and hope comes solely from him and there isn't a darn thing we can do to improve upon it. We surely don't deserve it and we will never be good enough to add anything more to Jesus' work. We simply place ourselves under his love and grace – under the umbrella of his shed blood, which gives us the power of God to overcome sin. It's all him - all the time! His grace is poured out to undeserving people and every single one of us is undeserving. Ronnie and Dotty were in church that day.

Later that night when sitting in her bedroll under the Maple Street Bridge, Dotty said to herself, "Why not me?" Then and there she surrendered her life to Jesus. Over the next couple of Sundays, I saw something different in her. She wanted a new life, change, new things. She didn't want to be on the streets any more addicted to whatever high could numb her pain. She contacted a son in California and began discussing moving down there to be with him. Whenever I had helped her out before it was always with an effort to adjust this street living a little bit to make it easier or take care of some immediate need, but it wasn't for any substantive change. This time when she came to me for one more chance at help it was due to the desire to totally to get out of the street lifestyle.

She put me in contact with her son and we began to dialogue about moving Dotty and Ronnie down to his place. Her son had done time in prison for drugs and was now a played a major role, embodying servant-leadership values, in several groups of Alcoholics Anonymous (AA) through sponsorship (of others attempting to gain or maintain sobriety). He was recently married and had a little one, and with some fear and trepidation on his part we began to discuss terms for moving them down to California. A contract was agreed upon with stipulations of sobriety, drug testing, mandatory attendance at recovery meetings, money management, and, upon Dotty's insistence, mandatory church attendance too. I contacted a pastor of a sister church of ours that's only fifteen minutes from where they would be moving, and he said he would love to have them come. The Covenant branch offers Celebrate Recovery (a Christian-based 12-Step program) on Wednesday nights, AA on Thursday nights, and the church even has a homeless man playing bass on their praise team.

I put the word out on Facebook that if anyone wanted to help unite this family please send cash. I really didn't expect a lot because a month or two earlier when I had posted to raise some money to keep them from being evicted only two people responded. But in two hours we raised over six hundred dollars, from multiple people, to donate to fly them and their dog to Sacramento, just after the New Year. We would have gone sooner but there were other factors involved.

Ronnie's ID was out of date. "Do you think that's going to be a problem at the airport?" He asked. Ronnie has never flown before and never even stepped inside and airport. We had to fly them because of the dog. Greyhound won't take animals and Amtrak was too expensive. I had to make an appointment to get him a new ID. "The dog hasn't had any updated shots either," he added. We looked online and found a veterinarian that would come down and deliver shots for about a hundred bucks. We made that appointment, too.

The next week I had a social event to attend downtown. At this little soirée, I met a girl who worked at Spokane Humane Society. "This could be a divine appointment," I thought to myself. We talked about flying dogs to who knows where and shots and what not and before the night was through I had a new appointment for less than half the original cost to get the shots and paperwork done for Ronnie and Dotty's dog.

"What about a dog crate?" I threw in, deciding to go for broke.

"Yeah, I can get you one of those too," she chimed. We ended up with a free dog crate that otherwise would have cost us over one-hundred dollars. We accidently came an hour and half early to our appointment when the time came but that turned out to be God too because the vet who was on duty that day was leaving early due to the holidays and we would have been unable to get the dog on the flight.

At every big and little turn, it felt like God was active. We were even able to put them up in a hotel for two nights before leaving so they could sort through their stuff and be clean for the flight. I helped them climb the hill to their spot under the Maple Street Bridge on Sunday Dec 30 to gather all their stuff and say goodbye to Spokane.

Dotty and Ronnie gave a public testimony to the church that very Sunday morning thanking God for a new start. They knew it wouldn't be easy, but they now had something inside them wanting to try this time. I would say that *what* is inside them is really, *who* is inside them– the Holy Spirit of the Living God.

It's all Jesus. We just hang around the right places long enough while proclaiming His truth and showing whatever love we can, as often as we have the strength and the means to do it. In some cases, like this, even when we're out of strength and the love has been exhausted.

At some point God reminds us all that anything of substance done will be done by the power of His Holy Spirit. It will be done, not when we say so, but when he says so. Real hope, real change, real transformation only comes from him! His grace is poured out unconditionally on all of us undeserving, crazy, hell-bent people who don't even see him wooing us most of the time.

Dotty's Words, used with her permission:

The last Sunday in November my pastor, Rob Bryceson at First Covenant Church, gave a sermon about how all you have to do is believe in Jesus. You don't have to be good enough or try to tip the scales by doing more good things. Just Believe in Jesus and nothing else. Things will begin to happen for the good.

That night I prayed the prayer that he told me to pray. My life started to change so quickly it makes my head spin. The very next day, my street mom was sitting with all of our stuff and all of the dogs while us kids all went to the store. We were gone a lot longer than we were supposed to be. When we got back we found out a lady had stopped and gave her fifty dollars and then asked her what she was going to use if for. My Street Mom said we were out of dog food and that she would give us kids a hot meal at Taco Time. And she did. Well, a few hours later two ladies pulled up and sat on our bed and asked, "What do you need?" The lady took all of our sizes for boots and jackets then went to Wal-Mart and probably spent a couple of hundred dollars on the stuff we asked for and even stuff we didn't ask for. I've been homeless off and on for over ten years here. That has NEVER happened before.

It was not too long before this, that Ronnie asked me if I wanted to still move to California to be with my oldest son - To get clean and sober and off the streets. He asked me if we would like to start anew life with me and my family there. I said 'Yes.'

The very next Sunday after I decided to believe in Jesus, we talked to our pastor, right after the church service. Suddenly things were set in motion. Our pastor took the phone numbers down of my son and called that afternoon. A couple of days later I talked to my son about it and he said yes, but that we would have to sign a contract and be clean and sober. We emailed each other back and forth until we agreed on a good contract. Our Pastor posted it on the internet on Monday afternoon and by that evening we had enough in pledges to pay for our relocating to California. This included our dog and everything! ALL THIS HAPPEN AFTER I GAVE IT ALL TO GOD.

I want to first and foremost thank Jesus all he is doing in our lives. I also want to thank the people who have given donations to help us to start our new life. It is not often when someone gets lifted out of life on the streets and is given a fresh start. I am overwhelmed with gratitude. I also want to thank my friends at First Covenant. You have been encouraging us through the past three years and have stood with us and never stopped believing that Jesus could make a difference in our lives. We made some poor choices along the way and we are so sorry for any trouble or disappointment we caused by those decisions. Thank you for believing in us and for being here to point us to Jesus. Please continue to pray for us we still have quite a journey before us.

    Love Always,
    Dotty

We flew her, Ronnie, and the dog to unite with her family in California. She's moved a bit since, but is still a Facebook friend and is doing fine.

27. I WOULDN'T HAVE THOUGHT OF THAT

Doing downtown urban ministry I was constantly confronted with issues and ethical decisions for which I have had no previous training or practice. I was constantly discovering there are policies and procedures we need to put in place that make me say— "I wouldn't have thought of that."

How drunk can you be and still come to church? That was a legitimate discussion question at a meeting of our usher/greeter team. What precipitated the discussion is that a few Sundays back we had three totally wasted guys come to church. They snuck in during the adult Bible study time at 9:15am, and had sat overly comfortable in their chairs (if not totally passed out) during the discussion time. But somehow when they shuffled down the hall to the church service they became increasing loud and active.

It was awkward because our usher team doesn't really show up in force until the main service starts. And that particular day all of our "big guy" ushers were inadvertently not scheduled to serve. By the time the ushers did show up in force, at least two of the inebriated had been participating in some kind of church activity for over an hour. Some of our team considered it a little hypocritical to tell them now they couldn't come to services drunk. So, there was some pause in taking action.

"They didn't cause any problems in the Bible study," I would hear later. But mind you this is a group where in the past we have considered it spiritual progress for some members to stop using street profanity during the discussion time. Everyone has a different starting point.

I was caught off guard when one of them stood up wobbly at the back of the house and gave me a one finger salute using both hands during the sermon.

You might not know this, but that can be distracting and cause the concentration of the speaker to go adrift. I figured demons just ain't ever gonna give ya an "amen" so I must have been preaching pretty good that day.

That was unlike a few weeks later when someone sitting up front was rolling paper cigarettes during my message. If your congregation is rolling smokes during your sermon – you've lost them and you're not as good as you think you are. If I ever teach in a seminary I shall share that bit of wisdom with my students.

At our usher/greeter meeting we decided: *Tipsy is Tolerable – But Sloshed Gets Tossed.* Every church needs pithy little memorable slogans to live by. That's one of ours.

Because of one of the other totally tanked participants we discovered another rule to live by in church. *If You're Going to Wear Saggy Pants that Fall Down in Back - Underwear is not optional!* Someone should probably put that in the weekly bulletin. I wanted to put it on the reader board outside, but cooler heads prevailed.

Thanks to drunk number-three, we can also safely guide our guests: *If You Take a Bite of a Cookie from the Tray After Service, there's No Need to Put It Back—*
Please Know You May Keep the Whole Cookie.

"While we're at it," one elder chimed in during the meeting, "what about the shopping carts and dogs?"

It turns out that one of our church problems is finding the best place to store shopping carts and overly large backpacks during Bible study and church services. This was another dilemma I wouldn't have thought of during my seminary training. The dogs really aren't a problem. They are more behaved than some of our other guests, but their hair on the pews is hard to vacuum off. *Dogs Must Stay Off the Pews, Please! – Blankets for Your Dog, which can be Placed on the Floor, can be Provided upon Request.* I wouldn't have thought of that one before either.

I was also recently asked if I could perform a baptism for someone – with her dog. I hadn't thought that would ever come up. I have no problem baptizing her, but I'm certain her dog doesn't need it.

As the Scripture states in Romans, 8:19-22, "For the anxious longing of the creation waits eagerly for the revealing of the sons of God. For the creation was subjected to futility, not willingly, but because of Him who subjected it, in hope that the creation itself also will be set free from its slavery to corruption into the freedom of the glory of the children of God. For we know that the whole creation groans and suffers the pains of childbirth together until now." (NASB)

So, I think animals are awaiting the full restoration of humanity in God. The hope of the dog lies in the owner's redemption.

I'm glad she didn't have a cat. I don't think you could ever baptize a cat. Just you try, and you will see they are indeed–the devil's creatures.

We couldn't decide yet if our guests unplugging and turning the electric liquid Glade air fresheners upside down to dab the contents on their person is a good or bad thing. It makes us go through the costs of air fresheners faster than our budget allows but perhaps there is a greater benefit we simply don't appreciate yet. That decision was tabled for further review.

Several weeks after inebriation Sunday, I met a clean cut and well-groomed gentleman during our meal who informed me he had attended church totally wasted a few weeks earlier. I remembered him and his fingers.

When I asked where he had been lately he told me that he got jumped while sleeping outside and someone had kicked in his ribs and broken his face by stomping on him. When he woke up in the hospital he hadn't remembered anything, only that he had a new metal plate in his face now. He was living in the Veterans Administration recovery home and going through treatment for addiction, working on restoring his life

So, if you were wondering... there is a God.

28. GOD WATCHING

One of my best childhood memories was when I was five or six. My addict dad got in a rage again and was beating my mom with a beer bottle when my mom grabbed me and ran outside. We slept outdoors that night; I think it might have been on the neighbor's lawn. As we lay there looking up at the stars, my mom, who couldn't speak very good English pointed up at the stars and said, 'See those stars? You are going to shine like one someday.' I knew in that instant that she loved me, and she was doing the best she could. But she simply didn't have the skills or ability to be a real mom.

Katie said this to us on a Sunday morning, when asked to identify her best, early-childhood memory with a perfect matter-of-fact, straight face. We had been working out a series of sermon dialogues on Sunday mornings, which we called God Watching. We were calling it that because, through the stories of people in our congregation, we were looking for signs of where God has shown us that His hands have been on us throughout our lives. At the same time, we were looking for signs of where God is moving people beyond their pasts. It was quite a ride listening to these stories.

Katie and I sat down on Sunday to dialogue about her life. Katie is the one who had come to us a couple of years previously as an abandoned street kid who had just turned 18 and been dumped by her adoptive mother at the local woman's shelter.

"Have a nice life!" her mother called out to her as she drove away.

A couple days later, Katie was invited to our church by a homeless man who often attended our services and helped out. For the first time in her entire life she walked into a church to see if God might be there to help her. Although at the time she didn't even know it was a quest for God she was undertaking.

Katie tells a great story of how God took that moment and then worked her over for the next couple of years to bring her to saving knowledge of Him. She speaks openly of her rebellion and final surrender to Jesus Christ during that time. She became our nursery director for a short season, finished her associates degree at the local community college and left us to jump to Seattle Pacific University where she planned on pursuing a degree in teaching, childhood psychology, or early childhood development.

A week before that, on Mother's Day, a beautiful African American member of our church, named Lindsey, was interviewed by one of our leaders on what it was like growing up dirt poor on the wrong side of the tracks in Oklahoma City. Her mom held the family together in spite of ghetto level poverty and a drug addict father. The power of the church and prayer held a family together long after it should have disintegrated.

She remembers being struck with death threatening childhood asthma. Her drug addict father was stealing the saved-up money for her medicine, so he could go out and buy a fix. Her mom with bravery beyond belief went to the drug dealer's house and demanded the money back and got it! Prayer, faith and desperation met in one instance of outstanding motherly heroics to save a child.

We also interviewed another woman who had been coming to our church after seeing a news story on our homeless meal Super Bowl Sunday. She works for the radio and TV station and was compelled with her boyfriend to come and check out a church like ours, which would do such work. Her story is painful to hear. She grew up in small town in Montana in a very poor family with both parents being philandering alcoholics. Her father would disappear for weeks on end and mom would drop her off at a local church on Sunday mornings with a baby brother and a diaper bag. Mom wouldn't pick them up again until 6:00 pm. She was barely old enough to just be in elementary school at the time. She and her brother wandered the streets with nothing to eat but the extra cookies she stuffed in her pockets at church. No one ever helped or said a thing because the grandparents were well to do contributors to the church — though not attendees.

Her home was violent, and she carried that expectation of violent love into every relationship she ever had. She would eventually become an informant for the FBI and DEA on breaking a major drug ring her abusive boyfriend's family ran.

Her first attempt to discover God was derailed by a Lutheran pastor who wanted sex in exchange for baptism. Why she came to us and stayed is beyond belief. But God doesn't quit!

It's amazing sometimes to hear the stories of God's successes. These stories weren't coming out of our homeless community meals; they were now the stories of our regular church folk. Well, regular to us, maybe not for most churches. The starting points of life are often so far down we would write these people off as never having a chance. If we take the time to listen and learn, we often discover hope through others. In those times, we discover that God is indeed watching out for us!

In an authentic church, people get to tell their real story. They get to be both who they once were and who are they are now at the same time. Most of my church world didn't so much like the past stories except for testimony times that could draw cheers and attendance at a service. But such stories certainly were not for church leaders and key laypeople. In the end, it's not who we were, not even who we are that has any real substance – it's who we are becoming under the hand of Jesus.

Since the time I first heard all three of these stories above there have been many more twists and turns of the journey. Two of them I no longer see or know. One has moved away. In each season of our lives, in each moment we are called to be faithful to who and what is in front of us, first to Jesus, then to others. As we do this we learn to be faithful to our true selves too. The self we don't have to hide, the self that struggles and doubts and sometimes rails against life and God himself. The person we are now and the person we are becoming often fiercely battle each other. Many times, we are confused about which side to be on in that struggle, aren't we?

The African American woman, Lindsey walks with Jesus. The woman who grew up in Montana and was an FBI informant, I never see or hear about any more; she was once a good friend. There is pain there for me to even write that. *(Sigh)*. That's the reality of church.

The last time I heard of Katie was on the six o'clock news. She had gone to SPU, spent a couple of years there, and then returned to her tough family and rough friends. She made the six o'clock news here because she was found half clothed in a dumpster one morning with her throat slit. She had refused a sexual encounter with an acquaintance. He beat her senseless, cut her throat with a box knife and stuffed her in a dumpster. But Katie lived! Believe it or not, she walked away from that too.

I believe God still has big plans for Katie, I know His hand remains on her life in spite of present circumstances. I hope I get to see the final place of glory that I still believe He is going to manifest in her, and through her, and with her—the same as he is doing with all of us.

Life among the walking dead of the lowest rung of society has its own pitfalls. The contagious infection of sin continues to permeate the air and none of us are immune. *God save us, all.*

SECTION 5: THE SAFETY ZONE IS COMPROMISED

Salt and Light

You are the salt of the earth. But if the salt loses its saltiness, how can it be made salty again? It is no longer good for anything, except to be thrown out and trampled underfoot. You are the light of the world. A town built on a hill cannot be hidden. Neither do people light a lamp and put it under a bowl. Instead they put it on its stand, and it gives light to everyone in the house.

> Matthew 5:13-15 (NIV)

29. I LIKES TO SITS IN CHURCH

I had one of those conversations again. It's the same introductory statement I've heard made by hundreds of people over the years. Somehow the topic of church came up and I asked the young couple across the table where they went to church.

"We go to Mega-Church," the lady answered sheepishly. "We go because we can just sit, nothing is expected of us. We really like Pastor's preaching though," she added, as if to justify her answer.

Actually, "Mega" isn't the real name of the church but you can use it as a good substitute, because I've had this same conversation with many people in different locations over the years. The answer is often the same. "I like the music," or, "I like the pastor's teaching," are statements that suffice to explain their presence there. The add-on, "I can just go and sit," is the troublesome part for me.

What I find interesting is that many these people are long time Christians who have been saved, discipled, and trained at some *other* church. They got involved and found the level of burnout to be severe, the absence of appreciation to be scandalous, the lack of meaningful relationships to be sorrowful, and the intensity of church politics to be sordid.

Now they are purposefully picking a church to attend where the main goal is to remain detached and isolated as individuals. They just want to be part of an unnecessary crowd attending the most entertaining venue on Sunday morning.

I get it at one level – believe me I know the nature of church, but at another level I don't get it at all. Many of these people are at the stage where a Christian's maturity should be moving them into influential leadership positions, where their years of study, testing, and sacrifice should be allowing them to be entering their most fruitful years for the kingdom of God. But then they pick *mega-church* exactly because they don't have to do anything, and no one needs them they contribute as little as possible personally, except for maybe a tithe check which they hope someone else is putting to good use. In essence, some of the most trained and practiced Christians are choosing a church where they aren't needed at all.

When and where did we ever get the idea that the creation and purpose of the church, which Christ instituted to advance his kingdom on the earth, should be a place where we personally are totally unnecessary and detached from others around us? Why do we think church should be just a place where we are spiritually entertained? I mean, why bother going at all if that's all it is?

In reading a New Testament a person would never, *ever*, get the idea that the church was to be a place where I can go and just sit. Pick any of the Epistles and read it. You will find that the purpose of the church is to unite a community in love – often a love that needs to be polished and refined through difficult processes. It's supposed to be a place where the love of Christ is poured out into the heart of an individual and then united in a group in such a way that the very existence of the Holy Spirit on earth working through people can be seen by the world at large. The reason that we aren't whisked immediately off to Heaven upon conversion is that we each have a long way to go, as we are being shaped by the relationship process, under the Holy Spirit's orders. As we do this journey – Jesus wants us to greatly impact others around us with love, justice, mercy, and righteous action!

"Oh, someone else does that part," you might say.

But we study the Scriptures to create action; it is to be "useful for teaching, rebuking, correcting and training in righteousness, so that the servant of God may be thoroughly equipped for every good work" (II Tim 3:16, NASB). We gather for the sake of heartfelt worship. We gather to express our deepest longings, joys, pains, and hopes to God. We gather to intercede in prayer for others. We gather to praise the majesty of his name in a corporate voice. We gather as influencers of others, as people who share Christ's love with others lifting their spirits and helping to carry their burdens.

The church is supposed to be a fellowship of real relationships united under the power and guidance of the Holy Spirit. Church should be a place of ultimate belonging to a genuine family requiring a level of authenticity, trust and support on a deeply intimate level. It was never supposed to be an entertaining show where classroom programs substitute for kingdom building action. The very thought that one could pick a church based on the power of its entertainment while remaining personally detached would be bizarre to the Apostles.

When I was kid I remember a popular poster of a cartoon character perched on a stump. The caption read, *"Sometimes I likes to sits and think, other times I just likes to sit."* I wish more of us would at least sits and think when it comes to our church.

On Friday nights downtown in our church, Union Gospel Mission began coming down and serving grilled hotdogs or fresh sandwiches to the street people. They set up in our gym and often prayed over people while passing out needed clothing or hygiene supplies. They even did foot washing as they put clean, new socks on tired, dirty feet.

Their original idea was to reach out one ring further than the mission could to dispel rumors and stories that had risen among the street population about the mission itself. Since the mission requires passing a Breathalyzer to get in, they wanted to have a place to reach out where some of the rules could be laxer and they could work to invite men and women to the mission by building relationships first. Finally, getting to the place in life where going to the Union Gospel Mission is a viable option is a scary thing for most street people.

Friday nights often got church people who wanted to help. Once, a group of nice church folk from the suburbs came down to "help out." They didn't give any funds, they didn't want to make sandwiches, they wouldn't help set up, they didn't assist in cleaning up, nor did they talk directly to any street people during the evening. They stood about wanting to "observe" the work being done. I guess they wanted to be the Jane Goodall of homeless ministry, taking anthropology notes.

At the end of the night I was told the whole mission team and these nice church folks gathered in a circle to pray while holding hands.

"Thanks for allowing us to serve you tonight by being your hands and feet to the poor and downtrodden," one of these church people prayed - OUT LOUD.

Now I don't know what you think, but I believe if you're the hands and feet of Jesus you MOVE! You act! You serve! You touch! You get dirty doing any job that needs done. You don't stand around observing then try to pray some credit onto your poor, shriveled, wormy, anemic soul at the end. No! And I really do feel strongly about this, if you couldn't tell. It offended the regular mission volunteers too.

Contrast this to that same weekend on Sunday afternoon. At our Street Wise meal, a team of social media experts came to cook and serve our meal for the homeless. Most of this team did not attended church anywhere and were a bit frightened to walk into a church to help – especially the gay couple. But they put on a brave face and dared to help since their buddy Mike, who attends here, recommended us.

They worked like a harmonious team of bees or ants taking direction from my wife, Tonia while chopping and slicing, cleaning, sweeping, mopping, and standing over hot stoves grilling meat! They gay couple was completely flabbergasted at how our team of leaders treated them with unexpected love and acceptance as part of the team doing our Christian work. They were overwhelmed to the point of actual tears when dealing with the homeless people they met that day. One of them had never really looked at the face of a homeless person before much less talked to one.

A lot of conversation took place behind the scenes among these un-churched people with our leaders during and after the meal. One of the men holds an executive position at major hotel corporation. That day, I'm proud to say, Red Lion Hotels picked up the tab for the entire cost of the meal; several hundred dollars. What a contrast to the Christian volunteer team from Friday night. The gay couple asked if it would be OK to attend a church service with us knowing were an evangelical church. They used to be Catholic; of course they can come.

In Matthew 21:28-32, Jesus told a story about two sons to show how obedience to God really works:

'What do you think? There was a man who had two sons. He went to the first and said,' 'Son, go and work today in the vineyard.' 'I

will not,' he answered, but later he changed his mind and went. Then the father went to the other son and said the same thing. He answered, 'I will, sir,' but he did not go. 'Which of the two did what his father wanted?' 'The first,' they answered. Jesus said to them, 'Truly I tell you, the tax collectors and the prostitutes are entering the kingdom of God ahead of you. For John came to you to show you the way of righteousness, and you did not believe him, but the tax collectors and the prostitutes did. And even after you saw this, you did not repent and believe him.'

John the Baptist preached a message of repentance for the forgiveness of sins. Mark begins his gospel with the words of Isaiah, The Prophet: "I will send my messenger ahead of you, who will prepare your way" – "A voice of one calling in the wilderness, 'Prepare the way for the Lord, make straight paths for him.'" (NASB)

I couldn't help but think of this parable when contrasting our righteous Friday night church people from the so-called *sinners* who worked and served Sunday afternoon. What does it mean to you to, to *make a straight path for him?* I think it's breaking down any social construct of injustice, offering mercy and grace to those who don't deserve it, and offering hope and healing to broken, lost, and wounded souls. *What are we to do with this ironic twist of reality?*

I was struck by how I personally had more respect for those whose hearts were moved to tears over the wretched state of the poor and who had a willingness to humble themselves to do any job in order to help; rather than those who refused to move an inch to make a contribution, but thanked God in prayer for being hands and feet of Jesus. *Which of these do you think did the will of the father?*

30. TO SAVE A LIFE . . . OR NOT

The City of Spokane, each year, asks for local business, non-profits, warehouses, and others, to submit requests to be a warming center during the cold winter months from November 1st through March 1st. These act as emergency shelters for the homeless when the temperature reaches seventeen degrees or colder. In 2012, *no one* applied.

We thought about it—a lot, BUT decided the 8:00pm to 8:00am requirement to open wouldn't quite work for us around some of our events.

We have minor kids here each Monday night for the youth symphony and there are several times during December alone where we are holding special services or banquettes that won't end by 8:00pm. In addition to this, two to four people need to be ready to spend the night in the church with up to ninety-five homeless men at short notice. It didn't seem very feasible. So, we decided it wouldn't work for us. We didn't put in an application either.

Since I had been a part of the Spokane Homeless Coalition for a couple of years, I've met many people in different levels of government or who work at non-profit charities. The city called me.

"Rob, no one applied this year and for the first time in a long time Catholic Charities can't pick up the slack on this one. Would you please help us out? Is there anything we can do to work with your church?"

I don't know about you but when the Department of Health and Human Services decides to call a church and ask for help—I say, "Don't fumble the ball on this one."

I went to work doing what I do best—making connections and thinking outside the box. After a flurry of phone calls, I called the city back and proposed an idea. What if we hosted the Warming Center but staffed it with Union Gospel Mission staff that could come down at a moment's notice and spend the night in the church? On any given night when we couldn't host the warming center due to schedule conflicts, we have a second and third location already predetermined to be the alternate setup. These sights would have to be within walking distance of our church. Central United Methodist Church just got a brand-new pastor, who was one day on the job when I called.

He said, "Absolutely!" when I pitched the idea to him. I liked him right away, not just because of this, but because he is the main announcer of the local Scottish Highland Games every year. We are blood connected in some ancestral way—I'm sure.

I had a delightful conversation with the more liberal woman pastor of Westminster Congregational Church, and she, too, promptly said, "Let's go for it! I don't know how our Board will react but let's get the discussion moving forward at least."

So, we planned on partnering with Union Gospel Mission and two other churches along with the city to provide emergency shelter to homeless men that winter. It was rather ironic that three of the oldest and poorest churches in Spokane were stepping up to help the community in its emergency needs. All three of us churches were barely hanging on financially and each of us were wondering how long we can last into the future under present conditions. Those other two are sustained by some money from endowments and we were borrowing from the equity in building. However, we were the ones at that moment in history and we care.

We care not just about our own reputations, but about all the things we think Jesus would do under these circumstances. Would Jesus save a life? You bet! Since it's in our power to follow the steps of Jesus, so will we.

The city plan was to reimburse expenses, so we had to make sure that each of the UGM Staff was paid for their nights of serving with usually enough left over to help offset paper product and cleaning costs for each church. I also called our electric and gas utility company and in a conversation with them they decided to help us with costs by donating $1,500 to us. No one ever told me how much wheeling and dealing there is to run a downtown broke church.

Creating partnerships and thinking outside the box is the only way to survive under these conditions and to get things done. But our church believes that this site belongs to Jesus and should be used in any way possible to do what Jesus would do and to speak what Jesus would say. It's not convenient. It's not simple. It eats up a lot of time that isn't under the classic church umbrella of activity. But Jesus owns our building and our commitment is to put it to the best possible use under his leadership. We thought Jesus would open the doors to save a life—so that's what we planned to do.

In the end, the Westminster Church Board was nervous about housing the crowd and the United Methodist Church couldn't pass the fire inspection. So, it was just us. We found an alternative sight for Monday nights when we were occupied by Spokane Youth Symphony and we waited for the cold to set in.

Several nights over that winter we opened for the homeless men to come in. It's amazing how many guys just won't go to the shelters. Some are kicked out and others just don't feel safe there or don't like mixing with the crowd. We saw an average of forty men come in every night that the city called to open the warming centers. We never had a single incident or mishap. The biggest problem was that the bureaucratic system was too slow to respond to the need and several times when the temperature dipped low enough to be open; it was too late in the day to make the call to open and I wondered where the men slept when it reached 20 degrees.

The upshot of it all was that the following spring I got to play a role helping rewrite the rules and regulations on the cities warming center policies and procedures. Much better planning was the result and the minimum temperature to open the facilities was raised significantly.

I continued to be overwhelmed with the fact that if the church just steps in to meet a need, God will open doors of opportunity that will result in much more compassion and justice for many more people over many more years. It just takes someone willing to start doing *something*. He will take care of the rest.

Think of it – is there anything your city or county government would ever call you or your church about in a time of crisis asking for your help? Would you fumble the ball if they did? Or would you do whatever it took to have the church make a difference? Who knows what the end results will be? *God knows.*

31. THIRD WORLD CHURCH IN A FIRST WORLD NATION

One Sunday my wife found herself sitting in church desperately praying not to throw up. I know for some people the thought of going to church makes them queasy and slightly nauseous but since she's a pastor's wife so that's only sometimes the case with her. A street woman who was a friend of ours came to church that day for the very first time. She had been coming to our meals for three years but had never been to a church service, even though she called this her church and called me her pastor.

She came this day because her on-again-off-again boyfriend was dying. His cancer had come back with a vengeance and he was lying in a hospital bed that very moment with no hope for recovery. We didn't know during that church service, but he would die that night.

Our friend had come to church in such a state of shock, worry and agitation, that we were genuinely concerned for her. She had obviously been out on the street for days and hadn't been able to get cleaned up or change clothes in quite some time. I wasn't sure if she was off again or on again with her last home either because my wife and I had seen her on TV one night in a news cast getting arrested for outstanding warrants while sleeping under one of the freeway bridges. She probably woke up under a bridge that morning too, guessing by her state.

She had come in early to service while I was rehearsing the band and staggered up to the stage for a hug as she cried on my shoulder. It was all I could do to keep my eyes from watering; the smell radiating off her was so strong. In fact, after she walked away, and I resumed practicing the worship, the smell clung to me like a vaporous cloud for the next ten minutes.

All during church, she sat in tears, resting her head on my wife's shoulder and wrapped up in her arms. That's why my wife was praying not to throw up. The stench was overwhelming, and she wanted so bad to be there for our friend and not spoil everything by throwing up. During prayer time, this woman wanted to offer a prayer to God for her boyfriend and so she half-walked and was half carried by my wife to our prayer wall.

We put up poster boards on the sides of the sanctuary and at any time during the musical portion of our worship service anyone can get up out of their seat and go write a prayer request. Other people go around during the service and pray over the prayer wall. We put up eight to ten poster boards and they fill up every three weeks or so. Whenever I'm feeling sorry for myself, I often go prayer the prayer wall to get my bearings back. I always walk away grateful for my life and family.

Thanks for not letting me be successful in my suicide attempt, - Please take care of my kids who are in foster care and help me get sober so I can one day see them again, I love them so much, - God please help me stay off meth, I'm so scared and don't want to live like this anymore, - Jesus please help my friend who is facing eviction because she lost her job when her boyfriend beat her and she couldn't make it in to work. —These are the kinds of prayers you might read every week on our prayer wall. The prayer wall is usually people's first attempt to reach out to God. They will write prayers long before they ever sing a worship song.

On that Sunday, our friend stood for some time before being able to scrawl out a prayer. My wife had to hold her pen hand to get her started in writing a prayer. I think it was her very first time trying to reach out to God on behalf of her dying boyfriend.

Sometimes our church is like a third world experience.

"You just need more tithing members to join your church" was the advice we recently received from someone about how to make our church a success. Yeah, we know. But how many Christian housewives do you know who live in the middle class of a first world nation would willingly go to church every week in a third world experience? How many of them do you know who would even potentially be in the position to hold the hand of a street-woman whose boyfriend was dying of cancer, let alone spend their church time desperately praying not to throw up from the proximity of the stench all during the church service? How many churches would have let that lady in and how many would've let her stay? Yeah, we just need more middle class first world people who willingly go to a third world church every week to come on down and hang out with us; should be no problem.

I don't doubt for an instant though, that Jesus would hug and hold the smelliest of us during a time of crisis or pain. It never crossed my wife's mind that there might be an alternative action like simply avoiding contact with the woman who was desperate for hope and love. There was never a thought by anyone to ask her to leave - Jesus wouldn't.

At our last board meeting the discussion took place about the smell of people coming to the adult Sunday morning classes. It's getting cold, so we can't open the windows anymore. Can you imagine little old ladies sitting next to homeless people who smell of the street while helping them find verses in the unfamiliar pages of the Bible? We have that. The board decided we should buy several sets of brand new sweat suits or running warm-ups to offer people who have been on the street too long.

"Seems like you've had a rough week," we would say to them. "I can tell you've been through a hard and difficult time because the street is still on you. Would you like a fresh change of brand new clothes this morning? You can use the restroom to wash down and change and get a new start today. There's even a bag for your current clothes until you get a chance to wash them."

If we had the money, we would convert the old unused men's restroom downstairs to showers. Wouldn't that be a nice touch? Get cleaned up, wash that suffering, pain, and hardship off you, change into this new stuff and come worship Jesus with us. Everybody is welcome. People are accepted, and lives are changed, but it takes extra effort will, patience, endurance and cost.

Third world church in America must think differently than first world church. Most first world people would prefer a church service where none of these things is even a consideration. But where is Jesus in our suffering world to be seen today? Who would Jesus hang out with and what personal price would he pay to be there? In each moment, we are all deciding where and how we will show Jesus to the world around us. Sometimes we even get it right.

32. STRANGERS AND ANGELS
with Reese McMullin Holford

The following words were written by one of my non-Christian, atheist-leaning friends. She is a social worker and we have often talked about where we might see God in this world if He was really there and we were ready to see Him. She posted this on Facebook once and gave me permission to use it.

In the very few and far between moments I get to myself, like the drive to and from work and the early morning showers before the sun and children have risen, I get to think about the irony of humanity and the strange walls we put up between us and others. In these moments, I giggle to myself about the absolute absurdities of the 'whos' and the 'whats'. I think often about my self-sacrificing ancestors, both alive and dead. I think often of the strangers I meet on the dirty streets and in the lines of suburban organic market places and main stream pizza joints. I think about the differences between the man who cut in front of me in line at Starbucks and the man who stumbled and tripped his way across the street this morning. You see I know, and this is a big secret, I know they are more alike than different. I've never traveled overseas; I've never seen an ocean different than the ocean that licks the shore of my childhood. I'm not well traveled and even less well schooled, but I know secrets that some well-traveled and well-schooled don't . . . I know there is no difference between the well dressed, well paid man with an agenda and a timeline and the un-bathed, ignored man with nightmares and delusions. I know we are all just here and we are all just angels being entertained by strangers. Some days, you are the stranger and some days you are the angel. I know that no matter your holy book, lifestyle, or net worth your blood still knows your hearts trials and your tears still know the red inside of your lids. We are all strangers and angels on the same day. I don't mean to offend my religious friends by using a biblical reference, nor annoy my atheist/agnostic friends. It's just on very rare occasions I get an urge to remind those around me that we are all the same strange mess, with different faces.

I responded on her Facebook page, "I like it A LOT! - that quality you call 'angel' I call 'the image of God,' placed in humanity at creation (Genesis 1) and dignifies every living soul!"

It's because we believe that we aren't so different from each other that we love, down here in the trenches and gutters of Spokane. It's why we still pray for God to act on behalf of those who have raged against him, why we still hope in hopeless situations, why we see beauty in the ruin of broken lives. The image of God resides in all of us and at all times there something of great value there to shine through the mud and dirt and filth of life, even if it's wearing a three-piece suit, a Vera Wang gown, or Goodwill hand-me-downs. There is a soul that Jesus loves so much he would die for it. As long as breathe is drawn, God isn't finished with the story of each person.

What Christ calls his followers to do is look deep into the heart of others searching for that image of God which longs to be set free. This is the good news Jesus wants us to tell those in lofty positions, and low: *There is a God in Heaven that knows we aren't different from each other, that we are all strangers on this earth longing to find our home, that we are all secretly desperate and sick with pain and sorrow, that we are all criminals who deserve punishment but ache for freedom.*

Oh, if only there was hope that in spite of all that has gone wrong, in spite of all the *should-have-beens* and *could-have-beens,* and all of the *if-onlys,* that have plagued our existence and trampled us to despair; *if only* there was a power big enough, loving enough, and strong enough to overcome it, all. A power that could set the wrongs right, could dispense ultimate justice while showing boundless mercy, could make up for all of our shortcoming and repair all the damage we have done and that which was done to us, could rescue and bring back to life all of the *too-lates* and all of the *never-beens* and all the *used-to-bes* and all of the *never-weres.* If such a love and power truly existed and was within reach of every living person, wouldn't that be the greatest news in the history of humankind?

If someone ever found that love, and knew it was readily available for every ruined life on the earth, wouldn't it be worth telling every broken soul she ever encountered?

Hebrews 11:1-2: "Now faith is confidence in what we hope for and assurance about what we do not see. This is what the ancients were commended for." (NASB)... And, 11:13-16: "All these people were still living by faith when they died. They did not receive the things promised; they only saw them and welcomed them from a distance, admitting that they were foreigners and strangers on earth. People who say such things show that they are looking for a country of their own. If they had been thinking of the country they had left, they would have had opportunity to return. Instead, they were longing for a better country—a heavenly one. Therefore, God is not ashamed to be called their God, for he has prepared a city for them." (NASB)

Hebrews 13:1-3 13: "Keep on loving one another as brothers and sisters. Do not forget to show hospitality to strangers, for by so doing some people have shown hospitality to angels without knowing it. Continue to remember those in prison as if you were together with them in prison, and those who are mistreated as if you yourselves were suffering." (NASB)

This is the message of The Gospel: Jesus Christ, the greatest love the universe has ever known. He stepped off his throne of godhood, disrobed his glory, and came to earth in human form. He lived to show us the heart of our Father God in Heaven and died a substitute death on our behalf for all the sins and pains and wounds we would ever commit. Love is found in bowing down to Him as He truly is, and inviting him to come within and to live inside us, each. *The invitation to a new life in Him is offered to all who would come to him and believe in His name.*

33. YOU JUST NEVER KNOW

One blistery cold weekend, as we prepared for our neighborhood meal, Tonia felt strongly that she was to use some of the Street Wise funds to buy a couple pairs of boots to give away.

"That's not really needed," I told her; "The Annual Winter Wear Drive, sponsored by another agency, is happening in our church in a few weeks and hundreds of pairs of boots will be given out then. You don't have to buy boots now."

Nevertheless, Tonia felt God wanted her to buy boots to give out. To keep it modest, she only bought two pair of nice work boots that were on sale, for about thirty dollars each. She bought what they had left – a size twelve and a size thirteen.

That Sunday afternoon, Crazy, one of our favorite homeless guys who often comes to church, told us he met a guy on the street who was new to town and only had a pair of flip flops to wear. All his other stuff had been stolen. Temperatures were already in the low thirties. It hadn't snowed, but it was very cold to be wearing only flip flops. Crazy brought the guy to our meal and asked Tonia if we could help his new friend find shoes. Smiling she told him to find me. Crazy introduced us. The fellow was a big guy.

"I just happen to have a brand-new pair of boots to give out to someone today," I informed him, stealing Tonia's credit since she was working in the kitchen. She is rarely wrong on stuff like this; when she says she hears Jesus, *she hears Jesus*. "It looks like this is your lucky day because we haven't had shoes or boots to give out in several weeks. What size are you?"

He told me he was a size twelve and had trouble finding anything that big. His eyes lit up as I handed him a brand-new pair of size twelve! He quickly put them on and tried to hide his discouragement when they didn't fit right. With a slump of his shoulders he took them off and gave them back saying, "I'm sorry but they're just too tight for me, maybe someone else could use them."

"Actually, we have the same thing in a size thirteen," I chirped like an eager Nordstrom's clerk.

He put them on and they were perfect! He must have shaken my hand and thanked me a dozen times before he left that day. I told him that it wasn't me but Jesus and Tonia who were the ones really taking care of him.

We didn't have a meal the next week since it was the first Sunday of the month and we had begun to cut back since funding was getting harder and were being a bit overloaded. Besides a few other churches kept crawling down out of the suburbs to serve meal s under the freeway a block away so their work was drastically affecting ours, undercutting our attendance and food costs.

It always bothered me that churches won't pick up a phone to call and see what's going on already, but I know since our building is old and tired looking they automatically think we're worthless, incompetent, and stupid, so they must come to the rescue of the poor forgotten homeless people in our neighborhood.

I've tried to talk with most of these groups, but I get blown off a lot. They all insist that Jesus is telling them to do what they're doing. So, I guess Jesus isn't very smart at business and efficiency. I guess he's always having his followers duplicate their efforts, waste labor hours unnecessarily, and double food production and costs. I guess Jesus must like over serving food in a timeslot where one local ministry has already existed for years while it struggles to keep paying the upkeep costs, and then having other timeslots during the week where no one is serving at all, so that the locals go hungry. Maybe Jesus doesn't know humans should eat every day? Some churches seem to think homeless people eat once a month judging by their outreach work. Other churches know because Jesus must have told them that one good Thanksgiving meal a year is all the poor people need to survive.

If I were in charge, I'd have all those suburbanite churches do some homework first and see there was an existing ministry they could volunteer at and financially support. But in my opinion, Jesus seems to be commanding his followers to do a lot of dumb and unnecessary stuff. I hate second guessing The Lord God Almighty, but it's apparent Jesus isn't good at logistics and communication either, I suppose; Because, we would prefer closing our Sunday meal and getting a break if fifty people are going to serve a hot meal one block away under the freeway every now and then. We would've happily sent our homeless crowd over to them had we known they were coming. Jesus doesn't think of those things I guess because he's always telling people to just go down and serve more food. We often dump discarded clothes and coats in our dumpsters because Jesus seems to have told a new church that the stuff the other church brought down last week, or the one the week before that, wasn't good enough.

I've often wondered why Jesus has one of those churches come down twice a month to our neighborhood when they have to drive through three miles of poverty and broken and ruined neighborhoods all around their church building to get to our area. Maybe Jesus doesn't know all those homes between us and them are full of despair and poverty and hunger. I doubt it's because the good church people don't really want those poor folks actually *attending* their services, although some of the homeless have told me that's what they think.

I do notice with one group whom we never know is coming the two times a year when they put on their big shin-dig that the local media always seem to know when they will be there even if we don't. The newscasters and reporters are usually there in force to report on their good work and increase their donations for the twice a year shin-digs.

If I were a cynic I would suggest that perhaps most of these works aren't motivated by loving the poor but judging by the church T-shirts and bus signs, are motivated by marketing pictures for their brochures when showing off their good works to newcomers and visitors whom they want to join their church. If I were cynic that is; But, I digress from the point of my intent for this story.

Two weeks later we bumped into Crazy again.

"Did ya hear what happened after you gave those boots to that guy? He went to a job interview the next day and got the job. The employer took such a shining to him that he found him a place to live too. He's off the street already! Thanks to you guys for all you do! That pair of boots actually changed that man's life!"

You just never know. We always tried to tell the people who read our newsletters and sent us donations, that those funds are used to buy food, blankets, reading glasses, and boots. Homeless guys who came to church felt safe to invite others and Jesus changed lives through the obedience of those who are willing to follow his lead even when it doesn't seem practical. We all played a role in letting Jesus use us to change a life. I guess this little moment kind of makes me eat my earlier words about all that church help which seems inefficient and poorly managed to me.

You just never know how much one or two small things can really help - even if it's only a couple times a year. Doing something I suppose is often going to go farther and make more of a difference than doing nothing at all, even if I do think we could all be a little smarter at our efforts.

34. TOILET PAPER AND HOPE

Just before Christmas, 2012, we sat down for a church staff meeting, to discuss our financial straits. There were three of us at the meeting. One was a volunteer board member, the other a part time administrator, and myself. We were now officially one and half years into using our equity line of credit to rebuild the church. We had decided to spend heavy upfront to fix up the building, get some staffing help, and give ourselves a good head start. We thought with success we could the borrow less and less as the next couple of years unfolded. It wasn't working.

By the end of 2012 we were failing miserably. We had grown to around eighty people but only half of them were sober or had a place to live on any given Sunday. Even the ones who weren't living on the street were having trouble. I had gone through many months the previous year where I was the only person on the board who still had job. That's right, through layoffs or retirement, except for me; my entire board was unemployed as we exhausted ourselves trying to figure out how to build a church.

We lost people who grew discouraged or tired of the type of church we were and the kinds of people who came. Unless God was going to do an advanced miracle, we were without much hope. The going was slower than we have hoped.

We had recently had a Sunday offering of $325, total. That's right, and NO there isn't a missing zero. If we could add a zero to that total, we would be at the break even amount we need weekly.

At the end of November, we were depleting our savings and in between draws on our line of credit against the building. Our church treasurer had ordered a spending freeze.

At this particular staff meeting on a Tuesday morning we were literally discussing if there was enough toilet paper, paper towels, and cleaning supplies to get us through one more weekend. We thought there were. This is the deep stuff we dialogue when preparing for the busy Christmas season: "Do we have enough toilet paper to make it one more week?" It wasn't alarming to us, just something on the check list.

I had to confess, sometimes it's hard for me to see where Jesus is moving and sustaining us in our work. I know I should have more faith. Everyone told me so. But discussions of toilet paper were never urgent concerns at any of my previous church positions, so I found myself confused at interpreting God's motives and plans for us.

Usually, during Christmas time, churches are ramping up their plans and rehearsals for the huge Christmas pageant and vast crowds that will be coming in, not discussing how much toilet paper they have to make it through one more Sunday.

Later that same week a woman came to the church door with a jar of coins. She and her kids had been saving them to give to us to help the homeless. She knew about our church because a year earlier I had written a comment on the blog site of Donald Miller, the author of *Blue Like Jazz* (2003, *Publisher:* Thomas Nelson). The woman with the jar of coins had read my response which I had posted on the comment section of one of his articles about our church situation and was stunned to learn she lived in our same town.

For the previous year, God had laid us on her heart. Every time she drove by the church, which traffic studies showed 47,000 people a day do at our major intersection, she prayed for us and thought to herself that she should try us out. But it takes working up some courage to drive to our neighborhood on a Sunday morning and walk into our building. We understand. She told us she had attended every major large church in the Spokane Valley for the last several years, first trying one then another looking for a place to fit. It wasn't working, and her restlessness was increasing.

As she handed over the jar of coins she said, "The final straw was seeing my church's budget. Every year at this time, our huge church posts its budget for the next year and when I saw that we are going to spend $36,000 on toilet paper I just couldn't believe it. TOILET PAPER!" She practically shouted. "I just couldn't do it anymore," she sighed, "it seemed so excessive." I was certain other paper products must have been included in that total.

That's when she told us about God speaking to her for over a year about trying us out. She had no idea how what she just said echoed in my heart and head as we stood there talking. Toilet paper seemed to be the theme of the week. I thought about how two churches only miles apart in the same town in the same state in the same country can be living such incredibly different existences. It's more like we are living in an entirely different civilization than they are. I couldn't help but think that somewhere in the deprivation of resources and essentials there is a parallel to Joseph and Mary.

At the time of Jesus' birth, Caesar Augustus was sitting on the throne of the Roman Empire as sole ruler of the world. New military campaigns and conquests were being put into motion and a census was moving thousands of people around the empire. Millions of dollars of goods were traded and shipped across the Middle East and around the Mediterranean. Wealth was pouring out across Europe, North Africa and Asia Minor. In Judea, Herod was partying while planning and building glorious palaces, even as he plotted whom to kill next. Architects and engineers from Greece, Rome and Egypt were working on a rebuild of God's Temple in Jerusalem just a few miles from Bethlehem. This was a project that costs hundreds of millions in today's currency and would take forty-six years to complete. All this was going on while one young couple mocked for her early pregnancy were journeying to Bethlehem with no fanfare whatsoever.

The simple expectation is that a young mother would have her own mom, a midwife, and family about her as she gave birth for the first time. She could expect to be in a known home that provided shelter, wisdom, and support. A new dad should expect to be surrounded by his friends and the celebration of the young son should be a huge community event. The expectation was not that they would be deprived of the most basic of items at such a crucial time. No one assumed that they would discuss where to move animals and where to place the baby after cleaning out the manure from around them first. No one prepared for a novice dad instead of a midwife to be the one there to pull the baby out, cut the cord, and place the child in its mother's arms. No one assumed that even the simplest of things like buckets of water for cleaning would be hard to find. No one wanted to feel alone, afraid, and helpless at such a time. That was certainly not the expectation of where to find God.

And yet – in all that vast contrast of the Roman Empire, God came to us in the small cave that was deprived of even the most basic of needs and expectations for a baby's birth. God didn't come in the wealth and majesty of the Caesar's Rome or in the splendor of Herod's new Temple. He came to a young couple living in poverty, deprived of even the most basic expectations.

Maybe God still comes in places trying to figure out if they have enough toilet paper to make it through one more week. I suppose the question is, "...When he does...will we see him?"

After sending out this chapter in a newsletter we saw a significant shift. Two couples who had been reading our newsletters finally caved in to the Holy Spirit's prodding and joined our church. They would both become significant leaders in ministry and the course of action that was coming would not have been made without either of them joining us.

We also received an incredibly generous gift from Shoreline Church in San Clemente California, pastored by my friend George Hulse. In the five years that we ministered downtown among the poor, only two protestant churches ever made a donation to us. Individual protestants did, but not churches. This gift, and two from the local Mosaic church, meant a lot to all of us working in zombie land. Thanks to all of you who kept us going!

35. BLOG COMMENTS AND A JAR OF COINS

Donald Miller (2011) had written a short story about how being in church was like going to dental school to learn all about teeth and how to do dental procedures, but then never actually getting to open a real mouth and look in and do the work for which he had studied. I thought the point was that church was incessant school learning without any useful or practical action (that actually helped people). But my overarching impression was that Don blamed the church leadership for this problem. So, I posted the following in the comment threads which would eventually bring that jar of coins to our back door.

I read the parable and almost all the other comments. I pastor a downtown, poor, urban church of eighty people, half of whom are homeless, addicts, and prostitutes, and others of equivalent reputation; it's a tough neighborhood and tough ministry.

I have found most Christians don't want to "graduate," rather they like to just look at the "schools" we choose to attend. Nice places with new carpet, a coffee bar, playground, excellent band, and a new lighting and sound system; millions spent on creating a certain ambiance. Then, we complain about what the schools don't do. Truth is – each student could choose a school where they are needed and not where they're tastes are catered to, but we don't. We blame the school, not ourselves.

Every Sunday we feed 150 people in a free meal at our church. Do you think we can get Christians to come and sit and share a meal with the broken and lost and wounded of this world? Just to have a meaningful conversation with one of them? – Hardly.

Mostly, there are only two or three of us in the room. I've had a lot of Christians visit, but not stay. They go back to the shiny happy schools by choice. Graduating means we must get dirty in the spit and blood and pain of "dentistry." Truth is – as much as we won't admit it – the majority of us just don't want to do that.

Don: The question isn't really what's wrong with the church; it's what's wrong with us? I've been in professional ministry for over twenty years in six different settings, denominations, and church sizes. I'm as guilty as any for creating the current church paradigm. This urban thing is new to me and its kicking my spiritual rear!

When we complain about "the church" do we really mean our pastors, board members, seminaries, and key leadership? We seem to have expectations that they should be doing something else with us. Like we're helpless and it's all their fault.

We switch churches to find more depth and meaning, but often just go from one popular, trendy place to another; swapping McDonalds for Burger King and complaining about the food quality and nutritional value. We want steak, but we keep going to all the same kind of burger places until we doubt that steak or grilled salmon even exist.

If there were no church buildings in America and all we had was the Bible, we would pick it up, read it, and then go down to urban centers, oppressed neighborhoods, or local trailer parks, because here exist the broken, disheartened, and poor. We would do this because we would KNOW that is where Jesus would be. That's where we would find HIM!

But instead, by the millions, we go to popular large, nice buildings where thousands of affluent people gather and the expectations on us are relatively passive. Someone else does the praying, singing, reading, interpreting, and serving. We spend our time listening to a lecture, wrapped in a top-notch show with great entertainment value, surrounded by excellent programs catered to each individual in our family. The vast majority of us attend churches where we don't know a pastor and none of the pastors know our name. Then we gripe about not feeling connected, deep or getting to the real thing. It's not the church's fault – It's our own choices.

I have Christians come to help who say, "What do you need?" I respond, "See that table of guys there? I need you sit with them and *be* Jesus. Speak *His* words, see with *His* eyes, love with *His* heart, feel with *His* compassion, say what *He* would say, do what *He* would do." Usually the Christian leaves instead. I guess several years of listening to sermons and sitting in weekly home group Bible study wasn't enough training.

But God is on His Throne. The Holy Spirit is alive and well on Planet Earth. Jesus' plan is moving forward and there are *many* who are still partnering with God in his work! The universal church is doing fine!

36. CAN ANYONE HELP?

I was standing in a trendy little downtown bar with a group of people sipping chardonnay and speaking with local government officials about the state of homelessness in our city. I was describing our Street Wise work and spouting off my limited wisdom of what I had been learning over the last several years. There were fifty to sixty people that evening and the whole place had been reserved for a private party. A non-profit agency from the other side of our state which works in political advocacy for the homeless was hosting the party. It was a post-election gathering and two state representatives, a state senator, several city officials, business owners, and numerous other leaders from non-profit charities working with the poor, were gathered.

The group sipped wine, ate brie cheese and crackers and glad-handed each other on all that had been accomplished over the last year to preserve funding for the poor among the states tough budget decisions. This was a room full of powerbrokers who spoke in terms of millions of dollars as they discussed homelessness and hunger. These were the movers and the shakers who created and sustained programs all over the state. I was invited because of my connections in working with Spokane's homeless population. But I was in a room full of powerful people who cared about our work.

There were several speeches given about all the hard work we had accomplished together and more speeches about what was in store in the foreseeable future. Promises were made to work diligently and tirelessly on behalf of the poor and though everyone knew the next year would be harder, everyone was going to pull their weight and not let the poor suffer unduly if anyone could help it.

While the speeches were being made my phone kept vibrating in my pocket and I kept hitting the ignore button. As soon as the speech making was done and we were standing about making those crucial connections and introductions that can happen in such a gathering, my phone buzzed again. It was an urgent text from my wife to call her right away. She hates these social gatherings and wouldn't go with me so instead she was a few blocks away hanging out at the church getting some work done at 7:30 on a Friday night – waiting for me to quit schmoozing. I called.

"There is a homeless family who just pulled up to the church," she said; "Another charity sent them here. There is a young mom and dad in their twenties, with four little grade school and preschool children living in a van. They have been kicked out of her mom's house where they have been staying, because they got in a big argument about her mom's drug use and concerning her druggie-boyfriends coming and going at all hours in the home, with the kiddoes present."

It was late November and starting to snow. They had no cash and nowhere to go; hardly any of the shelters take families and when they do it's not so late in the evening. "Can we help them?" My wife pleaded.

"Hold on," I replied, thinking the timing couldn't be more perfect. Here I was standing in a room with some of the most powerful people in the state who really care about this kind of issue. They were all much smarter than I and much more familiar with what could and should be done. Some of the people in the room worked full time in non-profit charities doing nothing but help families just like this one. They would know what to do. So, in my typical, bold, and reckless style, I raised my voice to get everyone's attention.

"Excuse me! Most of you local people know that I pastor that big brick church on Second and Division, just three blocks away. I know this is odd, but my wife is calling right now, informing me that a young family with four little children just pulled up and they have no food, and nowhere to stay." I glanced out the big front windows looking at the giant snowflakes coming down and after a small pause added, "Can anyone help?" . . . . . . Cricket . . . . Cricket . . . . not a cough, not a shuffle. . . . . "OK, thanks anyway." I sheepishly finished and slinked off.

I grabbed my coat and headed for the door. One guy slipped me a twenty to help and one lady handed me a hotline phone number scribbled on a piece of paper, which had just been set up by the city for such emergencies. I couldn't help but think of the total irony of that moment.

I rushed to the church, met the family, and then dialed the hotline number - a machine answered. I left a message detailing the situation and the emergency. I then dialed another agency I knew that helps families and left a message there too.

Eventually our church put them up in the hotel across the street for the next three nights, using our special pre-arranged discount that has since been canceled. We supplied them with some food and gas coupons and gave them a list of everywhere they could get meals each day. I made sure they went to Salvation Army on Saturday, because they help families and that's where the hotline number led. The place I left the second message called me back the next day saying they couldn't help directly, because according to the new rules, I had to call the new hotline number and route everything through them.

The family came to church Sunday telling me Salvation Army had an eight-week waiting list. The hotline folks would finally call me back, four days later. They told me to get in touch with Salvation Army. "The system is broken," I thought to myself.

I spent weeks, even months, thinking about that moment. It was so pathetically sad and tragic and laughable and revealing, all at the same time. Talk about lifting back the curtain to see what the great and powerful Oz really looks like! Here was a room full of people who congratulated themselves on really making a difference among the homeless but in reality, were totally powerless, helpless, and ignorant of how to actually do a thing when it was right there only a few blocks away.

But I also couldn't help but think about how much of my experience with ministries in church has been like this. How many times have we celebrated church growth, but it really didn't grow by any of our friends. How many times have we cheered for a new believer coming to faith, or new baptisms, but it wasn't anyone we personally knew, and it wasn't anyone we led to Christ. Have we ever applauded ourselves for all we had done in missions or compassion ministries having success in our church, but we didn't make a donation? It often meant a collection given by someone else, sent to somewhere else with still some other person, actually doing the work. How many of us even now celebrate the work our own church does in feeding the poor, but we personally have never worked in the kitchen, donated a dime to buy food, or come down to eat with our neighbors and make friends?

Often, we think that if the church we attend does it, we somehow get to ride in the wake of other people's works and gain some credibility for ourselves. But when confronted with the personal reality one on one – when it's our turn to confront poverty or brokenness or meet a need or share the truth of Jesus, or even pray with someone - we don't know what to do—so we usually don't do anything. "The church will help," we think, which means someone else, somewhere else, will take action and responsibility for *actually doing* something. We just celebrate it later, as the church holds a party.

We will sip our chardonnay and eat our brie cheese and crackers (figuratively speaking) and pat ourselves on the back. But, if we take an honest look, if some darn fool holding a cell phone says, "Hey, you, longtime expert Christian – I got a person here on the line right now who needs what you say you are giving to the world – can you help?" We sputter and cough and hope someone else will respond to the need.

We are far removed from the realities of what we think we are doing and other people are way more important because they are actually getting the work done. Perhaps Jesus means it for each of us *individually* when he said, "*Whatever you did for the least of these brothers of mine, you did for me.*" (Matt 25:40). Perhaps when the sheep and the goat judgment comes we won't be able to blend in with the right flock, but we will have to be called out individually to stand on our own and hold our heads up to what we have contributed to the cause of Christ. Perhaps, every now and then, Jesus wants us to look long and hard at what we think we're doing, and ask ourselves - *am I really doing it?*

Several years after this incident, the city of Spokane united with Family Promise to create the Open Doors Emergency Day Shelter. This, in partnership with their Bridges Program, now operates 24/7. The program offers shelter, aid, and help transitioning to permanent housing and jobs. We are all proud to say we now have the right place to call for emergency situations like this one.

SECTION 6: DYING AMONG THE INFECTED

Therefore, I completely despaired of all the fruit of my labor for which I had labored under the sun. When there is a man who has labored with wisdom, knowledge and skill, then he gives his legacy to one who has not labored with them. This too is vanity and a great evil. For what does a man get in all his labor and in his striving with which he labors under the sun? Because all his days his task is painful and grievous; even at night his mind does not rest. This too is vanity. There is nothing better for a man than to eat and drink and tell himself that his labor is good. This also I have seen that it is from the hand of God.

Ecclesiastes 2:20-24 (NASB)

37. CHANGE, IT'S THE ONLY CONSTANT

For over four years our church leadership teams had seen change, change, and more change. We would sometimes get lost in past ways of thinking that no longer fit the present reality, but we didn't know what to do that would make any significant difference.

Visitors from out-of-town would often drop by our church and comment about how dynamic and powerful the church service was, but then ask in a confused manner, "Why isn't this place packed?"

In my first four years, I think we went through eight or more board members who just couldn't handle the responsibility and stress of trying to hold onto (and fix) a dying church whose best ministry was with dirt-poor people. Working among the walking dead of zombie land was brutal on everyone. Only one member of the board made it through her whole two-year term out of the *second* group of board members elected since I'd arrived. None of the first group survived through the apocalypse.

During a discussion of a topic one of our new board members was caught off guard by some of our reactions to an idea. We'd been there, tried that, failed again.

"I have to keep reminding myself that you guys were planning on closing just last year. This church doesn't feel at all like a dying church. I know, I've been in a church that closed," she exclaimed in a manner, like a person remembering the world outside our doors had radically changed. We couldn't apply old strategies to life and living.

Our chairman spoke up saying "Yeah, this is the healthiest, most vibrant, alive church I've ever been in. We're just broke that's all."

We're just broke that's all. And that means change was always in the air. The future won't look like the present. It simply can't. But each week we asked ourselves what is the most important thing to do today? What does Jesus want to happen in us, with us, and through us today? After all, no future is certain for anyone at any time. The only certain thing we can hold on to is faithfulness to Jesus in the moment we are in. That's all we have. This means being faithful to come to services with our hearts honestly praising God in worship, faithful to pray with trust and hope on behalf of others – not just for ourselves – faithful to honor and obey his word in our daily living – even if others around us don't, faithful to build authentic relationships with each other that are honest, that inspire and challenge us to be more than we already are, faithful in any given moment to stand up for Jesus and tell his story of redemption and hope to lost, hurt and confused people whom we encounter, faithful to get dirty serving other people and not look for personal praise or applause when doing it, faithful to be generous with our money and our time for his kingdom's purposes, faithful to not give up hope that all of this still matters to Jesus and to us.

We're just broke—that's all— which means our congregation can't collect enough on Sunday mornings to pay the bills. Knowing that, we always knew something had to change. We just couldn't ever grow by enough people to stabilize. It didn't really matter how good church services were, or how often people said they, "felt God's presence."

Usually, that last comment came to us from out of area visitors passing through town. Some of them literally drove by and stopped, others found themselves staying at the hotel across the street and still others were seeking out the local denominational affiliate in town while visiting relatives or on vacation. Our church was one of two possible choices for that last group. The other church has since closed.

For the first two and half years we were always going to close "in less than a year," if the trends continued, unless we did something dramatic and drastic to change directions. Oh, did we ever try. I remember being at a conference once with a group of pastors and being asked what my plan was for the church and for myself.

"We will just feed people and tell them about Jesus until we can't, I guess," was my only answer.

It sounded weak, pathetic, and incompetent to my ears, even as I said it. But I was rather at my wits end. I found myself getting kind of mad at God for showing up so mightily in services. It would have been easier to dump the whole thing and move on if Jesus would quit showing up.

Around the same time, we were sending Dotty off to live with her son, and Jesus was having me use my trailer to help move a homeless lady I didn't like, Street Wise received a donation of fifty dollars, along with the following letter:

> *I wanted to include a little note with this donation. Over Christmas, my daughter and my husband attended one of your services where a few people gave their stories about living on the streets. The subjects discussed led to some great conversations afterward, but also really compelled her to want to do something to help people in our town. She has such a large heart.*
> *When I asked her if she wanted to give part of her*
> *Christmas money to our church or world vision or something else, she decided that no, she'd rather send all of it to you guys to continue the ministry that you are doing there in Spokane.*
> *Just thought you'd like to know. Not only are you improving the lives of people in Spokane and showing kindness to those who need it most, you are also making a difference in our life. I'm excited to see what she does, as she gets older, to better the world. Thank you for being Jesus to your neighbors and thank you for inspiring my little girl. Keep up the great ministry. You are making a huge difference!!!*

At the same time this letter was arriving in Spokane, I was at a conference in San Diego where, through an incredible coincidence, I met the husband/father of this story. He came up to me beaming as he vigorously shook my hand and gushed his "thank yous" to me over and over.

"Great! You're welcome!" I said; then, "Um, just what exactly did we do?"

"When my daughter and I visited your church, your worship leader, Brian spoke about his hard life during the sermon. And that homeless couple got up to give a testimony—the one you were sending to live in California with her son?" He reminded me. "Your service was so raw and authentic and the people so genuine. Some of the things said were not the kind of things we ever hear in our church from the platform. You guys are rather ...earthy." He finished trying to find an appropriate description.

"Oh sorry" I said, "We don't really mean to be—it just kind of works out that way, given the people we have coming." I didn't want to shock him too much by telling him we hear the "F word" a lot in our church—and, no, I don't mean *Forgiveness*.

"No, No," he assured me. "It was great. After church, my daughter and I went to lunch and we got the chance to talk for hours about major life issues, family, marriages, and all kinds of things that I have never had the opportunity to discuss with my daughter. It was ground-breaking for us. I'm so glad we visited with you on that particular Sunday."

He sighed with the relief of a man who got to have a major breakthrough with the child he had long wanted to speak with about deeper matters.

"My daughter was so taken by what she saw and heard that I think it helped point her in a direction for her life. It was fantastic." He exclaimed; "It changed her total outlook on life and for Christmas this year she got a lot of money for a kid and decided it was worth it to give most of it away rather than simply buy more junk for herself. I won't be surprised if she ends up a missionary one day."

"Really?" I asked; then said, "That is so great to hear how your perfectly timed visit ended up being so profound for you and your daughter. Would you do me a favor? Would you ask your daughter to write us a letter explaining her gift to us? (At the time, I had no idea her mother had already done that, and that Tonia was reading her mom's letter at about the same time I was having this conversation with the father in San Diego).

"No problem" he responded. "I'll ask right away. Whenever we come to Spokane you can bet we're going to be visiting your church." He beamed! Here's her letter;

Dear Members of First Covenant church,
I went to your church for the first time in late December while I was in Spokane visiting my grandparents. While I was there, I

heard a few stories about people who trusted God—no matter what happened to them. I thought about how selfish I was being for having all these things that I didn't even need while others barely had enough to survive. When I came to your church and saw how you worshipped God without the need of all the extra "things". It made me think again about what God's love is all about. I thought, "God doesn't care about our looks, or if we are rich or poor, what he cares about is what we have to give," Once I realized this, I wanted to give more than I usually do to charity. And I thought your church was a perfect place to start. I donated about 85% of my Christmas money to your church, to help people who have less than I do.
Thanks for all you do.
      Emmy— 10 years old

38. LEATHER COUCHES

One day my wife and I went to a relative's funeral at a really nice church. It had a fantastic view of their new building from the street, when pulling into the parking lot. When walking into the tall glass enclosed lobby, the new carpet smell was euphoric. Tonia stood there just inside the door for a moment breathing deeply and gazing about.

It didn't just have lights, it had chandeliers. Off to one side was a coffee bar and barista station with modern bar stools and tables. A top-notch information booth composed of wood and metal stood at the center of the lobby. It was adorned with extremely professional graphics and brochures. Scattered about the area were couches and coffee tables arranged in semi-private sitting areas. The carpet felt luxurious even under our shoes. It all smelled new and looked expensive. The other side of the lobby held a dedicated lounge with large windows enclosing it. The lounge was for new people to greet the pastor after church services.

Tonia kept making whispered, "Oooh," and, "Ahh," sounds under her breath, like a person eating a high-priced steak dinner at a classy restaurant after having only fast-food for weeks.

As we walked across the lobby I had to take my wife's arm because I think she was in a dream state walking in a floating kind of way with the grace and purpose of a Disney princess. The look of delight and wonder on her face was inspiring. Her mouth remained slightly open in awestruck admiration as we part-walked and part-waltzed into the visitor's lounge. It had a gas burning rock fireplace casting a comforting glow across teakwood tables and leather couches.

"Oh," she gushed, "Leather couches! They have leather couches!" She spoke with delight in a sighing kind of way like she'd entered her personal heaven, then added emphatically, "Why can't we have leather couches?"

Taking her firmly by the shoulders and turning her to face me I gazed into her beautiful green eyes and, with all the care of a doctor giving a diagnosis to an oblivious patient, said, "Because this church never has to worry that one of their visitors will come in so drunk he passes out on their leather couch and poops his pants."

Yes. We've had that happen. It wasn't on one of our nicer goodwill pieces of furniture though. It was on a wooden pew. I guess that's how they got their name in olden times. He came into a meal and passed out drunk on one of the pews we had lining the gym walls. I was glad we didn't have carpet.

Normally I would have done what most anyone working under our conditions would do; grab him by the ankles and gently drag him outside, even if he was over six feet and probably weighing in at 225 pounds. But I was thwarted from accomplishing my plan because the poop had run down his pant leg and into his socks. This prevented me from be willing to grab his ankles; so, I was forced to improvise a new solution.

I did what any thinking person would do, and I called the fire department because . . . I was pretty sure he was... *injured*. {Wink, wink}. At least, he *smelled* injured to me. But, then again, I'm not a professional and can't be sure I could properly identify gangrene. {nudge nudge}.

"God hates us," was my wife's summary of our life and ministry after her experience in the leather couch church. It was the little stuff like that which kept us from attracting people who would stay with us and grow our ministry.

It was the middle of Summer 2012, in our second year of borrowing from our line of credit, that I knew we were failing and we weren't going to make it. Sure, the ministry to the poor was doing well and there were great stories to tell. But I could do the math and for all the investment in the building and the increase in ministry programs, we couldn't grow enough to even get close to being healthy. We kept hemorrhaging finances.

I was told that this church ran a deficit budget for dozens of years – long before my time here. In the past, someone usually died leaving a big chunk of change for the church to limp along. This is how they had been covering the deficit for years. After working at the church for just over four years, we had one month and one month only, where the income matched the outflow of money. Every single one of my other fifty months we had lost cash – usually several thousand each month. For my first two years the cash from the previous administration's sale of the parsonage covered those losses. After July 2011, our equity line of credit with our denomination covered it.

When our board first sat down in December to lay out our 2013 Budget, it looked as if we would run a $60,000 deficit. I could hear the flushing-swirling sound of my own personal morale going down the toilet. Nothing we were doing was working. Nothing we tried made a bit of difference. We had spent $140,000 of our equity line of credit over the last few years and we needed another $20,000 to get through the upcoming year. The denominational leaders were now coughing and sputtering. We realized the $200,000 equity line wasn't going to be that much after all. I didn't' blame them. We were a lost cause.

Our church board decided to once again reach out for a consultant to help. We met with some regional denominational leaders who stared down at their feet and talked in the respectful whispered voice of a mortician selling a casket. They didn't want to outright advise us to close, but had no belief in us either.

"Well," one of them began after clearing her throat in that, now-here-comes-the-bad-news, kind of way, "You just have to get more people to come here and give." We were awestruck by her sage counsel.

"You're just going to have to decide what you're going to do," another added in the same tone as a doctor reading a Do Not Resuscitate order to the family standing about the bedside.

With little hope and no ideas, we quietly put the building back up on the market to sell at the beginning of 2013. If our church shut down, this would have to be done anyway and the process takes many months, so it was time to get it started. I called the real estate agent the next day to get a plan together and we put the sale of the building on the agenda of our church's upcoming annual meeting scheduled in a few weeks. I was hoping that with any luck we could wrap this ministry up and close her down in six months or so.

In the meantime, I spent the next few weeks looking over our scrawny, anemic and sickly budget. After crunching a ton of numbers, I discovered the treasurer had not included a big chunk of change in a separate savings account when giving us the paperwork on our budget. By whittling the last remaining expenses down, here and there, coupled with wildly imagining some creative income ideas (which meant more contract leases renting out our space and rooms in our children's ministry, for things like band practice rooms) I found a way to get that $60,000 deficit down to under $25,000. Only a twenty-five-grand deficit! That's do-able, I thought. With a boost in some nontraditional income strategies, we finally figured out we could get that deficit down to nothing.

For the first time, in my fifty-one months as pastor of a poor downtown church, we actually had it within sight of being a break-even year. But it was going to take extra effort. We finally had the potential of borrowing nothing and not selling anything to survive. But it was going to take a lot more than what we had been doing.

It was going to be the last ditch, do-or-die, desperate, breakout attempt to survive *in zombie land*.

We never had a lot of tithers here – still don't. That's people who give ten-percent of their entire income. About eight to ten individuals and couples cover the vast majority of our giving income. For a couple of years, behind the scenes, I was wheeling and dealing like a real estate mogul. I knew that all we had was our facility and we had to find ways to make it work for us. I thought our strategic, high visibility location would be ideal with the right investments and the right ideas. I went to work networking whomever I could.

A farmer's market was going on across the street, and I knew that would make our parking lot desirable. I had called the local representative for a large corporate entity, which manages parking lots across the country. We met for coffee and worked out a deal to share parking lot revenue. They would manage it for $100 a month fee and then we would split all proceeds beyond that 30% to them and 70% to us. The problem was our lot was poorly striped and only had 30 spaces. I met with a couple of companies who stripe lots and they weren't sure they could improve on that. I had them give me a copy of the codes and sat down one day calculating dimensions and square footage. As a musician, I can't tell you enough how outside-the-box this was for me. I found a way to get sixty spaces out of the same area. We did the deal and I got a company to repaint the stripes for a couple hundred bucks and donate the rest of their expenses. We would make several thousand more each year from a lease deal with our parking lot.

I was constantly negotiating and promoting ways to get rental income to groups like, The Youth Symphony; or, I was drawing up contracts for renting band rehearsal space, or we hosted special outside events to raise rental income. I was doing just about anything I could. Several times I got grant money through Street Wise, and we used as much as was legally and ethically possible to pay things like heat, water, and garbage.

But even with all of those it was not enough to cover our costs. It seemed like for every deal I made, giving dipped, making it a neutral gain. One year, I negotiated over $20,000 in those kinds of contracts. I had no administrative support, so I wrote out all the terms, contracts, and agreements myself.

I learned a lot about business, nonprofit tax laws, and real estate contracts – skills my seminary education never once suspected a pastor would need. I was always told by my professors, "You will have other people on your board that will do those kinds of things."

No—you won't. If you are going into ministry and reading this, I guarantee that you will need to know how to read a budget spread sheet and understand small business finances—especially if you end up in a small church.

Small churches don't get leather couches—even if you don't think people may poop on them.

39. WHEELING AND DEALING

For our new budget for 2013, I had to go back to the creativity barrel again. We came up with four new ideas to raise income to get us through the year:

1) Lease Advertising space on the backside of the building facing the freeway for $500 per month. This would be a giant 8'x18' banner with an add and a caption saying something like, 'Thank you to *such-and-such company* for helping us care for Spokane's homeless.'
2) Fix up two of our many vacant rooms in the upstairs area to rent at $300 each as furnished transitional housing for Union Gospel Mission graduates who are at the stage of preparedness to leave the mission and start a new life. There were agencies who could assist with subsidizing that rent. We also had connections solving legal occupancy issues on that one.
3) We started the Two-Dollar Club: fifty people who committed to donating at least two dollars per week, every week, in the offering plate. This includes our homeless congregational attendees who want to see our church and meals continue. That would add $5,000 to the total income for the year.

4) We added the Forty Dollar Club. We planned to recruit fifty people, mostly from outside our church, who would donate forty bucks per month, for the year. We also needed ten people in the current congregation who weren't giving at all to give at least forty dollars per month. Every church has people like that. If only ten of the existing people could find four friends who believe in our work in this neighborhood to agree to chip another forty per month, each, we would add another $24,000 to our year's income – then we could finally make budget!

If we could achieve these four goals in addition to keeping what were our current tithing and leases, then for the first time in many, many years we would not run a deficit. We could reconsider selling off our location. We would not have the threat of closing hanging over our heads anymore. We thought this was possibly within reach, but it would take someone being the champion of each of these strategies. Champions working on getting people to join one of the clubs or spearheading fixing up the rooms for rent, or working on getting the sign space leased.

We asked people to use their friendship networks and Facebook to recruit others to come and check out our church. Many of us had people who supported our work from far and wide and if we all just asked, then it's entirely possible that we could find our work here supported by hundreds of people who simply believe in a downtown urban mission field. Crazier stuff has happened.

Keep in mind this was all funding just to keep the church going with stripped down operational budget. All of the money and financial resources, which were used to run our Street Wise Ministry meals to the community, were raised totally outside of the church budget. This meant that we were raising, upward of, $30,000 *more,* to make the meals happen.

I had become a decent grant writer and used my connections at the Homeless Coalition to learn all about that process and get training wherever I could. I wrote grants to the Health and Human Services Department of the city and received $10,000 a year for two years in a row along with an additional $20,000 grant to remodel our kitchen. I have no idea how, really, we did it.

God supplied the bulk of the giving through my extended family and out of state friendships who believed in us and in our work. Some of the volunteers who came and worked in our kitchen became regular givers to the Street Wise Ministry, but the church was never able to give to it – other than supply the space and equipment – which was nice.

The church was never affluent enough to give anything to help cover those meal costs. In fact, when the poor started coming to church in the mornings and eating all the cookies, drinking all the coffee and pocketing all the sugar packets, we had Street Wise fund the entire church budget for those supplies, too. When the church still struggled, we had Street Wise pay $300 - $500 per month to the church for the offsetting of utility costs.

My wife ran the Street Wise meals and had to raise her own, part-time salary. Almost all of the Street Wise income came through Tonia's and my personal relationships; a few more made the list, through my business connections or my grant writing. Several other names also made the list, because they were getting our monthly newsletter articles or had read a recent newspaper or local magazine interview. We just weren't stupendously good at expanding that base.

The track record of people in the church helping raise additional funds was a pretty poor one. We kept donor records of, approximately, one hundred donors; of the list, usually all but four to five of these were friends and family of Tonia's and mine.

I must admit, I was a touch suspicious that church members would help raise cash even as we were getting ready to present our budget ideas. But, we had to try.

Imagine after all the extra effort of fund raising, and income strategies, sitting down and *still* needing to raise much more to keep the church afloat. It was exhausting. I must say that it was only Jesus doing it because it kind of defies logic and intelligence, doesn't it? How did a little broke church with barely any people and a not very good pastor who had no staff pull off this ministry at all and keep a church going with no resources? I don't know.

But at the beginning of 2013, I thought the basic four ideas to get solvent were pretty good. I announced to the board members that I would not be championing any of them. I felt I had done enough fund raising and thought it was time that someone else needed to take on those projects. I was probably more than a touch across the line on burn-out road.

For a while, we saw at least one hundred dollars per week come in spare change through the offering via the Two Dollar Club. The homeless stepped up. Some outsiders began to send us forty bucks per month, as part of that club. But in truth, we didn't get the church champions we needed for any of the four ideas. Someone needed to monitor the giving clubs and report progress. Someone needed to be able to say, "We only have twenty people giving in the Forty Dollar Club and I have an idea to get another thirty people on board." But, no one ever looked at the data or kept track and no one ever tried to write a letter campaign or do anything to get those clubs to happen. The homeless did pretty well for a while in their two dollars per week giving. But a champion needed to find ways to encourage and thank them and get more of them to join in and no such champion arose.

We didn't get the two rooms ready to house homeless (which churches can do legally under the national emergency shelter laws) because another church came along and offered to rent us for a Sunday night service, on the condition that no one be on site or housed in the facility. We thought that would offset the income and might end up being better for us in the long run, so we inked that deal, instead of developing the room-rental idea.

As we began 2013, we had a plan that had potential to work, but would take a lot more effort from more people if the venture was going to truly succeed. I wouldn't know until that summer, but the plans would be unsuccessful. In the end, the ideas were good, but proved failures in execution. We just kept sinking.

I cannot tell you how extremely stressful and frustrating it is to have to do three times as much as any ministry I'd worked in only to produce one fourth of the result. The constant stress and failure and discouragement will wear a person out. I decided that I wasn't a very good pastor at all. I couldn't really figure out how other guys did it and they always made it sound so simple at all the conferences I attended.

It was pretty obvious by now that I simply didn't have what it takes, *whatever that is*. I began telling Jesus in my prayer life that my path was one big mistake and I was way off track and began to ask Him what I was supposed to do to get out. Whatever I was supposed to be, this wasn't it. You can't keep failing and not realize one day something is terribly wrong, so it must be you. I started taking medication for high blood pressure that year.

40. PARACHUTING IN

By now everyone knows the colloquial definition of crazy as someone who keeps doing the same things the same old ways, expecting different results. We certainly aren't crazy because we have tried all kinds of new things and approaches to problems from all sorts of different angles. Unfortunately, up to now, we've kept getting the same results. So, I guess we're only half crazy.

The life of a church is a living organism and growth is mandatory for living things to exist. Sometimes that growth is above the surface were everyone can obviously see the change and other times it is below the surface where only those who know where to look can see it. The central change that we had been chasing for some time was that we need to grow in attendance and participation from resourced people.

We mean people who have the emotional, spiritual, and life skills to pass on to others in teaching, training, and guiding. We needed people who have the social and business connections outside of our church to help those who are "un-resourced poor;" and, people who have the funds to tithe and give to support and sustain the ministry of this church. In short, we needed to be at a minimum attendance of about 175 on Sunday mornings, to have enough of a mix of people to sustain us, but we were still only half that! The attendance growth can't just keep being an increase from the homeless population or the marginalized and poor; the un-resourced, of our community – increased attendance needed to be "resourced" people.

Unless there was incredible advancement in the previously mentioned ideas to generate income, we wouldn't make it through the year. I could already tell by March 2013 that if present growth trends continued just as they had been – it wouldn't be enough to carry us into 2014. We had borrowed $140,000 over the past two years, to transform our building and sustain the current ministry. We knew we were going to need to borrow again just to cover our operating costs, unless a miraculous turnaround came in a matter of weeks. Initially, we only paid the interest on the loan, which was around $400 per month. In the next year, or two, we would have to start paying back the full loan and those payments would triple or quadruple. If we couldn't make ends meet under present conditions – how would we add that extra expense and make things work? We aren't the Federal Government, after all – even if we were kind of acting like them.

Our board had been very real in assessing our situation and had been real in presenting information to our congregation. At our Annual Meeting, in January, ironically at the same time that we were presenting our budget options for potential success, our board felt duty bound to inform the congregation that we had four choices in front of us this year, if we failed. There had to be a back-up plan in case our budget ideas didn't work in time. Something had to radically change, since our growth had not proven sufficient.

These where the four choices we thought were before us:
1) Sell and move: The questions remained, to where would we move? Who among our members would stay with us? How much would it cost to build out a new facility?
2) Share the site: The questions to resolve here are with whom and for how much? We had explored this previously, but the prospects didn't pan out.
3) Fund the pastor's salary from outside: Is it possible to create a community development corporation that could get grants or foundation support? Churches have a very hard time doing this in general and funds for pastoral work

are almost non-existent. It also takes up to a year or more simply to create a separate non-profit agency.
4) Go to a part-time pastor: This would mean finding someone new probably with less experience because I would move on and find work to support my family.

The board's concern was, "And how long would it take someone new (and part-time) to reestablish the connections and favor we currently have with the city, the local businesses, the non-profits in town, and the homeless and poor populations?" Frankly, we've been stumped on what to do and simply started praying for Jesus to show us what He wanted. The congregation voted to quietly put the property up for sale figuring if things turned around we could pull it off the market or turn down a bad deal. But if a wonderful offer came to us we would have more choices before us.

In the middle of February, a visitor stopped by the offices, mid-week, representing a large church plant from an area mega-church. The entity was a spin-off of the giant mega-church in Post Falls, Idaho, which at one time was touted as the fastest growing church in America. I was informed that the mother church had some fifteen thousand people at services in a town where the entire population was about thirty thousand.

This group had recently moved into a location way out on the north side of town. They were growing so much that they were already considering another location and wanted something near downtown. Their representative was asking if we would be interested in leasing our building to them on Sunday nights for a 5:30 service. Perhaps God was deciding that option number two of the four (share the site) was the one he wanted us to pursue.

After several weeks of meetings and negotiations, we agreed and signed a six-month deal with an option to extend, if needed. They only wanted six months, because our auditorium only sat 250 and they were sure to outgrow it in that amount of time. We agreed to allow them to start an evening service in our location which planned to launch on Easter Sunday of that year.

This meant we had to move our Sunday night AA group to nearby Westminster Church, because they could not easily change their time slot. The lease wouldn't entirely change our financial situation, but it would help a lot. We knew we would work out some kinks in scheduling and timing after our Sunday meals but, all in all, our leadership had a very good experience with theirs and we believed that they would prove an asset to our community, and to the kingdom of God in Spokane. After all, Jesus owns the site and he decides what he wants done here. So, we were trusting Jesus to do great things for both of our churches.

I admit it, I was totally wrong. For the longest time in working for church revitalization in a poor, downtown neighborhood, I had a theory. My theory came from observations that a small congregation just can't really grow in such tough soil. The obstacles to overcome in a downtrodden environment, in an area with a tough reputation, with extremely limited resources of people and income, make such a venture virtually impossible.

Everyone knows, for instance, that without young families, you can't get a church to stabilize, financially or socially. And yet, how do you grow a preschool ministry without kids – or grow an elementary program with only a few children? I don't know any parents who want to bring their preschool child to a church where there are no other little ones or where there might only be one other preschooler in the class. Young families like the energy of strong and bustling activity full of lots of other families with whom their children can play and learn. So, until we can have six to ten kids in the program, young families just move on to somewhere that already has it going. The same can be said for youth ministry, singles ministry, and many other smaller demographic group specialties. People like to meet and worship with others who are like themselves. Growing from nothing is difficult.

For four years, I had told people that I think one of the ways to survive in a downtown urban context is for a group of 100-150 people to parachute into an existing facility with all of their staff, programs, children's ministries, youth outreaches, and social networks fully established. A core group of that size could overcome the obstacles of trying to grow something from nothing.

They would arrive with enough energy, enthusiasm, strength, and resources to leap to the next level.

When their church offered to rent our facility on Sunday nights, I thought, "This is it. This is what's needed for success to happen here. 125 dedicated and committed people parachute into the neighborhood, to build and sustain a viable church."

I admit that I was jealous that they were going to succeed with all their resources and personnel where I couldn't. There were even a few private talks about whether we might move to Sunday nights, so they could have the coveted Sunday morning time slots to seat the large amount of people who would come.

After four months, they quit. People weren't coming. The neighborhood was too rough and dirty. The locals often act uncouth, savage. The guy stripping down to his birthday suit in the men's room to take a sponge bath was too much for them. We hadn't even had that one. The locals can smell bad, too.

First the young families quit coming and then the rest just began to fade. In four months, the 125 previously committed people had dwindled to less than half that number. I was shocked. Their church is so known around our region that they can write their logo in crayon on a cardboard box and set it up in someone's front lawn and one hundred people would probably show up. All that strength, support, and resources, though, weren't enough.

So, my theory proved wrong. Oh, I know, the evening time slot isn't the best, the facility wasn't designed to young people's specifications and tastes but, still, incubating the church for a year and then moving it elsewhere to accommodate the growth should have happened. But, you can't just build a suburban ministry downtown. One can't do exactly the same thing here that one would do in the suburbs and expect it to work. The only way that could be accomplished is by chasing off all the locals and preventing them from participating in church activities (or, for that matter, even being on the grounds). We opted not to go that route. Maybe we're dumb.

Tonia and I recently took a trip to Seattle to speak with some other churches who had a reputation working with the poor and homeless.

"You have homeless actually attending your services?" one young staff woman asked us incredulously; "We could never get them to come to church," she added.

Their church finally moved all its homeless work to a separate location about a mile away. Everywhere we went we heard the same thing: people doing homeless work don't actually have the homeless come to church, or be a part of the community, or participate in regular worship—nor Bible study. Homeless work is *outreach only* and stays that way – *out there,* somewhere.

But, we did it differently. We invited the poor, broken, helpless, wounded, feeble, lost, lonely and hungry to come and be a part of what we do. Either we are really something special – or we're just plain stupid.

Still, it sounds a lot like *Jesus' teaching,* even if we aren't as smart as other churches.

41. DING DONG

I was growing concerned, as attendance and giving plummeted in July and August of 2013. Of course, I always wonder what we're doing wrong, and I ask myself the reason that this experience isn't valuable enough for return attendance. Why do a third of our people just walk away? I thought September would reignite the energy but, in truth, it wasn't a boom. It wasn't even a decent pop. The September-return-to-church didn't happen.

On top of that the regular donors to Street Wise suddenly stopped sending in their support in August. We thought that might have been due to the fact that we weren't open for the month, but when September rolled around, nothing improved. By the end of September, we were down to around six hundred dollars in the account, just enough to fund three meals in October, and that's it. Attempts to raise support and contact our donor base proved fruitless. In a last-ditch effort to raise some much-needed cash for Street Wise, we were selected as one of several charities to enter a local car dealership's charity give-away.

Thousands of dollars were up for grabs for the first through fifth place finishers, who simply needed to persuade people to "like" the dealership on Facebook and then vote for their charity. Several of us, with hundreds upon hundreds of friends, each in our respective databases of Facebook friends, took to the infamous social media platform with the purpose of asking all of our friends and acquaintances to vote for us (via their Facebook accounts) to, hopefully, get some much-needed financial help. We didn't think we could be number one because homeless outreach can never compete with charities that help pets. Furry animals are much more cute and cuddly than a bearded homeless guy, but we thought we could land fourth or fifth. Even a last place finish at fifth was worth $2,500!

For weeks we posted, shared, liked, and begged our friends to vote for us. We couldn't even get three hundred votes. The final days of the competition we asked our congregation to please help us and push this effort on their social media sites since we desperately needed the income to keep the program going. On the closing day of the competition, we lagged far behind and well out of any money position. We lost—and lost big.

Some of us were frustrated, others sad; by some of our team who had tried so hard to rally their friends to support us to no avail, I must admit that there was more than a touch of anger. This is probably a testament to the quality of relationships fostered on social media sites. We each posted numerous thanks to all the friends who did vote, though, and we thanked the dealership for selecting us as one of the charities worth supporting. On Facebook, we read, over and over, the gushing "thank yous" to the dealership, from the winners who were each receiving thousands of dollars of assistance.

Tonia and I decided God was saying that it was time to quit. We would host the three more meals and then finish the ministry. It was kind of a bummer concerning timing, because we were just setting up to launch a Jesus-focused recovery ministry, on Sunday nights in October, following the meal time. I guess some things aren't meant to be. We also could tell that the end of the church was coming. We were dying as a church and it was just a matter of time before we closed.

Tonia began a search to discover what else she should do with her talents and skills. It was time to find a new job and discover what else was out there. We spent the weekend reading some books, which investigate one's soul, spirit, and personality, to see what she might do next. *Strength Finders 2.0* (T. Rath, 2007; Gallup Press: New York, NY) was one such book. After looking over her top five strengths and discovering ways to use them, she determined that they all were being used, to a great degree, in her present dream job at Street Wise.

We were in the middle of discussing this on the Monday evening following the online vote, when the doorbell rang. We don't get anyone ever ringing the doorbell, except to sell something; so, I begrudgingly got up to answer the door.

A young guy, in his twenties, was standing there and he said, "I've been asked to give you this for Street Wise. It's from someone who wants to remain anonymous," as he handed me a thick white envelope.

"What?" I said fumbling, "for Street Wise? Well, thanks so much; uh, what's your name?"

"I'm Chris, but I don't live around here. I'm visiting from Seattle," he answered; "I've been asked to bring this to you from the anonymous donor. That's all." He finished, turned, and walked away.

I brought the envelope inside and tore it open to discover a four-inch thick stack of twenty-dollar bills and a handwritten note, which simply said:

"Please allow this money to bless Street Wise. We are sorry you didn't win the car dealership's competition, but hold on to HOPE. God will provide. Thank you for all of your love and dedication to the people of Spokane."

It was unsigned.

Tonia and I had sent little flyers around the neighborhood in which we live, to get votes for the competition. This had to be coming from one of them. It was amazing and inspiring. This is what we would have received had we finished in fifth place. We immediately began making calls to spread the incredible news.

Everyone began posting and reposting online. Word spread like wildfire on our numerous Facebook pages. This time, the thanks were going to Jesus, not to a car dealership. As this was happening, several others were going to the Street Wise Webpage and making personal donations through our PayPal account. By the next day, we had over four thousand dollars.

Tonia heard Jesus clearly say to her that the work isn't finished yet. There is still much more to do. He told her how the ministry was His; it was in His hands, and His hands alone. The glory needed to go to Him, this time, and *not* to an ad campaign for cars. Had we collected the votes ourselves, we might have then said, "We did this by human effort and persistence;" But, *this* way, He assured us, *He* was the one providing and sustaining the work.

We've known for a long time that there really isn't a First Covenant Church without Street Wise and there isn't a Street Wise without First Covenant Church. We are inextricably intertwined, and, the mutual need and support between this church and this neighborhood outreach are such that one will not and cannot truly exist without the other. Jesus is creating a different kind of church here. Even though we seem small and weak, he continues to say that He has work for us to do and that His hand is on us, to bring that work to full completion.

I had been doing this crazy journey for too long. I was coming up on the end of five years of being at this bizarre little church which had no hope of life and yet kept on living. We were a zombie church in a zombie neighborhood and we were attracting zombie people. Almost dead, but not really.

I still find the math hard to add up. Our giving never matched our budget and we had lost several thousand dollars, each and every month except for one occasion, during all those five years. In addition, we somehow raised funds through donations or grants to sustain Street Wise to the tune of over $40,000 per year (or more), which was completely outside of our church budget. I don't have *any* idea how that really happened.

It was during this process of coming to what looked like the end of Street Wise that Tonia and I completely let go of any control, hope, expectation, or desire of what the future would bring. God could save it or kill it, breathe life into it, or suck out the last molecule of oxygen from it, and we were at total peace with whatever would be His choice. We felt the same about the church ministry.

It was as much curse to keep it going as it was to let it die, if we considered the overall cost to our own emotional health and happiness. We simply let go of the last threads of control after this little social media experiment. We just weren't going to try anymore.

People who visited us often described a sense that God's presence was here and that something profound was happening, even when we who are constantly immersed in the struggle no longer see it or feel it. I suppose he likes running us to the end of ourselves in order to discover HIM!

42. 125 AND . . .COUNTING

On October 28, 2013, our church turned 125 years old. We're one year older than the state of Washington. People began worshipping here when we were still a territory. That's a pretty historic achievement. I doubt we could total up all the hours of prayer, worship, Bible study, and messages that have been uttered, whispered, sang, pored over, meditated on, and shared since that beginning date – thousands upon thousands to be sure.

Over the summer and fall of 1887, a small group of families and single men slowly arrived from Minneapolis, Minnesota, and eventually decided there was enough energy and desire to form a Swedish Evangelical Church. This group was already part of the Swedish Mission Friends, a newly formed denomination that would later become the Evangelical Covenant.

They began meeting for prayer and Bible study in a little wooden clapboard place affectionately known as The Bachelor House, because of the several single men who shared the dwelling.

Eventually they outgrew the house and rented an establishment in downtown Spokane for church services. That place went up in The Great Spokane Fire of 1889, when virtually the whole downtown business district was destroyed in flames. Rent skyrocketed after that and the group was forced to relocate to the basement of a Unitarian church, until they could find a new location. Two moves later, they purchased the Second Avenue and Division property in 1905. The original cathedral was torn down in the 1940s because it was no longer safe to occupy. A new chapel was built on the same site in 1950, under the leadership of Pastor Douglas Cedarleaf.

First Covenant Church has seen a lot of change in its time; several locations, numerous name changes, twenty-two different pastors (not including the interim leaders), services changed from Swedish- to English- speaking, from hymns on the pipe organ to modern guitar tunes, and countless other cultural, spiritual, and social reforms, alterations, and adaptations. Numerous people became missionaries, or were called into full time ministry, while others trained and launched out to do new works for Jesus' kingdom. Suffice it to say, it's quite a legacy.

I asked some of the old timers, "When did things begin to change and the church start dying? Why? What caused it?" I did some research in the archives to discover that the church was booming in the 1960s, but by 1971 they began discussing whether they should close down. This topic of discussion did not leave the church for the next forty-two years. Several poor leadership choices in successive decades certainly didn't help.

"It changed when the freeway was built," one of the elderly ladies once told me.

A block south of our church, I-90 cuts through town like a concrete river, dividing the affluent South Hill from the urban blight of downtown. We're on the urban blight side. A whole neighborhood of housing was torn down to make room for the highway. Others sold and moved out after that, because the area changed too much with low rent apartments, homeless shelters, and boarded up property that had little value. The freeway was built in 1968.

Three years later, the church was on the ropes and going down. I think that development, combined with an inability of the established church to respond to the Sixties cultural upheaval left First Covenant reeling, trying to find its mission and calling, in a world that had simply changed too much for it to keep up.

For the first five years of my time as pastor, closing was an issue looming over us like an ominous cloud. Every year of my time here, but one (the Summer 2011), until Summer 2012 (when we were first funded from our equity line of credit) we were dying. Most of the time, we wondered if the church was going to make it past the next year. Every spring I've swept my back patio, cleaned up our yard, and wondered if I would still live in my house again at the same time one year from then. It's hard to build a church, and, create energy and enthusiasm when you ask yourself those questions, year after year. Energy, hope, creativity and passion just keep dying. Somehow, miraculously, we still stood. It hadn't been without its hardships. We hadn't broken, not even in our cash flow for years, but attendance was up—and we didn't even count the dogs.

Ten days before our 125th Anniversary, I was informed on a Thursday afternoon that we did not get the warming center contract for single homeless men that year. In the application I filled out, just like the last year, I stipulated that I had to find an alternative site for Mondays, due to our existing contract as rehearsal space for the Spokane Youth Symphony. It just wouldn't be good to mix homeless old guys with young girls and their clarinets and young lads with their violas. Because of that Monday night problem, we didn't get the contract. It was passed along to another place with a gym a couple of miles away, a place way too far for the walking homeless population to reach. I was bummed out because this was the first year they were going to make the warming center contract valuable too— twelve thousand dollars for a three-month season.

The following Monday, I was told that the Youth Symphony was planning on leaving anyway and wanted to get out of their $750 a month contract with us for the 2013—2014 season. They gave us an eight-page explanation on why they wanted out, seven of the pages had to do with the neighborhood and reasons that families were no longer willing to make it to our location (for example, the neighborhood population's behavior—and their mere presence). They basically gave us a full-length document from 170 affluent families composed of reasons that they won't come to this corner, even when they really want to participate in an activity. In two days' time, we lost thousands of dollars of annual income and we weren't even close to financially stable to start.

We always knew that our area was a significant challenge for us, regarding church growth principles. We have a strange problem; the number one reason existing people in our congregation like our church is because of our open and heartfelt ministry to the poor; "Where the rubber meets the road," as one man put it. Paradoxically, the number one reason people won't come to our church is because we have too many poor people hanging around... Um yeah, figure *that one* out. We probably should have just ignored Jesus' words about caring for the poor, like most churches do; but our neighborhood simply made that unfeasible.

The following day, totally out of the blue, we received an offer of over one million dollars for our property, entirely unforeseen, from a megalopolis church that had thousands of people and millions of dollars. They wanted to buy us, so that they could open a satellite campus in downtown Spokane.

We discussed it and decided this was from God. Our property had been quietly up for sale all year long and we had not received one reasonable offer. Several years earlier, we had tried to sell it and received only one offer, in a year's time, from a developer proposing half our asking price. Now, a Christian ministry was offering us almost our full asking price within months of us having to shut down otherwise.

It was time to sell and quit. Our county sheriff told me in a meeting I had with a group of leaders that our end of downtown was going to experience a severe loss when sold and closed. He was genuinely grieved.

We had served the poor and done it as cheerfully as we could, just as Jesus asks us, but we were just not strong enough to sustain such service under the present conditions. If we can't grow, we can't sustain any ministry, no matter how loving it is, or how compassionate it is, or how effective it proves. We were just too small. I was glad to say, we had broken down some of our own prejudices and false notions about other people, and about ourselves too. We learned a lot about the love of Jesus, which we thought we already knew, but really didn't.

Our 125-year-old church decided to sell our site. After all our work among the poor, we decided that success took many more resources than we had. Poverty culture people need more than a meal, a coat, and bit of advice. They need a lot of personal management in decision-making and understanding ways that middle-class life and values really work. Folks in poverty aren't like middle class people without money – they are an entirely different culture with different values and different decision-making grids.

Middle class people rarely really teach poverty people the unwritten rules about ways to get along, to "make it." We tend to offer them one chance to get out, and when they typically botch the opportunity, we write them off as belligerent or lazy, having never understood the actual cultural differences. Poverty culture people need to be mentored out of their situations and out of their mindset, which is self-defeating—and they aren't even aware of the sabotaging tendency. The case management for such mentoring takes more than weekly attendance at a church service or a Bible study.

I was frustrated from sitting in an empty 12,000 square-foot building all week long, waiting to fill it on Sundays in order to pass the plate and pay for it all. I thought there had to be a better way to use God's resources than the classic model of church ministry we are all used to following—in the good old USA.

Most of my life, in ministry, I would say that we as a church have built great meeting halls and then tried to figure out how to get people to hang out in them, outside of Sunday morning, usually not very successfully, even for those who are really committed. I wondered if it was possible to create a great hangout for believers and unbelievers, alike, and then do church in that space. The idea had been rattling around in my head for years.

At the end of 2013, we had an offer for purchase of our building, releasing us from all the hardship and failed experiments of ministry to the poor. We were, after all, dying. We agreed to sell our site to the multi-thousand-member, multi-million-dollar church, Mars Hill, of Seattle. The enterprise was under the leadership of celebrity, teacher, author, and pastor, Mark Driscoll. What could possibly go wrong?

SECTION 7: THE FINAL ESCAPE PLAN

For we do not want you to be unaware, brethren, of our affliction which came *to us* in Asia, that we were burdened excessively, beyond our strength, so that we despaired even of life; indeed, we had the sentence of death within ourselves so that we would not trust in ourselves, but in God who raises the dead; who delivered us from so great a *peril of* death, and will deliver *us*, He on whom we have set our hope. And He will yet deliver us, you also joining in helping us through your prayers, so that thanks may be given by many persons on our behalf for the favor bestowed on us through *the prayers of* many.

2 Corinthians 1:8-11 (NASB)

43. COFFEE IN TWENTY YEARS

In an odd way, there was this great sigh of relief in my spirit. My wife and I had spent tens of thousands of hours to keep ministry going and rebuild a broken church. There were also tens of thousands of volunteer hours from other key people who had committed with us to do this journey for the last five years. All our work had failed to produce a sustainable church.

It had taken two to three times the effort, while in a poverty culture environment, to produce less than half the harvest that I had experienced in my previous suburban ministry roles. Honestly, I was internally breathing a sigh of relief that I could just lead this church through a sale and then let it all go and move on to something else. The weight was about to fall off my shoulders—*if* I wanted it—and I certainly *did* want it.

I was having coffee with my friends, Bill (the church treasurer) and Jim (our Board Chairman). We discussed what we *ought* to do next and what we *wanted* to do next. In our denomination, as long as our local church exists we own the assets and can decide how to use them, as a church body. If we ever fold or close, as a church, then all the assets revert to the denomination. I was sorely tempted to just let the sale go through, close the church down, hand the big fat check over to the denomination and move on.

"It's up to you," Jim said. "It's whether you have it in you to press on, or not; if you say no, it's no."

As we sat talking, we laughingly joked about our little congregation, which by then had become thirty members, twenty street addicts, and four dogs. What do we do with them now? What was our ministry dream?

How many times in your life is Jesus going to put you in a position where he hands you over a million dollars of His money and, in effect says, "Here, now, go build My Kingdom"? I've been around a long time and I never knew anyone who had that happen. Jim, Bill, and I began to talk about the pros and cons of shutting it down or trying to do something new.

"Twenty years from now we will be sitting on a front porch as old geezers, reminiscing about life. Do you want to be telling a story about the time Jesus offered you a million bucks to go build His Kingdom, and you said, "No thanks," or do you want to tell about the time you tried and maybe failed?" I asked.

Jim laughed and said "Well, when you put it that way... I'd regret not having even tried."

"Me too," Bill answered; "I think that will be a much bigger sorrow than if we were to try, but fail."

Our choice to try and press on was made. But, what do we press on *to do?* Building another auditorium-style church in the suburbs with a large playground and nifty latte bar in the lobby didn't fit us.

More than a decade before I had lived in the San Francisco Bay area, I used to get away, down to Carmel, Monterey, or Santa Cruz, for times of personal reflection and devotion. During one of my get-a-ways, I headed to Santa Cruz for a two-day personal retreat. I was in a difficult church-plant situation at the time. There was a lot of emotional and social struggle, concerning the maintenance of my sanity.

Highway 17, the Santa Cruz mountains, wind and wrap, twists and turns like a fast-flowing river of black asphalt as it connects the South Bay to the pleasant resort towns on the mid-California coast. One of the first sights a person sees, when dropping down out of the mountains coming into Santa Cruz, long before seeing the beach, is a towering white-spired church, high on hill, to the right of the highway. It's perched on a ridge against a backdrop of green mountain forest like a pearl in a setting of emerald: Holy Cross Catholic Church.

I felt the Lord nudge me to go there so I took an exit and climbed through city streets until emerging into the plaza in front of Holy Cross. I parked, getting out of my car with my journal, wandered around the church and plaza, while simply trying to pray and listen. A tree-lined park sits directly in front of the church, with more buildings and businesses surrounding. The church dominates the view at the north end of this delightful little plaza. I sat on a bench and asked God why I was there.

"What do you notice," I sensed Him asking me.

Looking around, I was struck by the city design. The church site was over one hundred years old. The cathedral rests on the site of one of the twenty-one original missions established in California in the 1700s. The city takes its name from the site, City of The Holy Cross. I couldn't help but be struck by the city leaders' decisions to build their park in front of the church, at some point in the bygone past. It's a common theme in the United States: churches towering over the green park, in the center of the original town.

"There was a time when my church was the center of society," I heard the Lord say in my heart. "The park was naturally built here, because this is where people met and worshipped. Here, they prayed and fell in love and married. Here they responded to community emergencies. Here, they held meetings to help define how the society would get along. Here, they grieved and comforted each other. Here, they played and laughed and built community. Here was the most natural place in the city to build a park, simply because the church was here. This was the center of society."

I drank in the moment and thought of how far we have drifted in a hundred years. "Will it ever be that way again, Lord? Can the church ever again be the center of community in America?" I asked.

"Yes, but it won't look like it did in the past and it won't look like it does now. You can't put new wine in an old wineskin."

I spent the next few days meditating on those thoughts. Now, over a decade later, I was again faced with that memory, wondering how to take Jesus' money and try to build a new wine skin.

In the weeks that followed that coffee time with Jim and Bill, our leaders began to discuss what we would do if we had the chance to throw off all previous expectations and assumptions, and build a ministry for both the middle class and poverty culture. What would it look like if we retooled the design of the space so that it worked all week long rather than waiting around to execute a good event on Sunday morning, hoping to draw a crowd to pay for it all?

From my church planting days, I knew a healthy church needs a minimum of seven-thousand square feet to accommodate all its Sunday service needs, classrooms, and offices. Any less and it would always struggle to collect a large enough group to be self-sustaining. The question we faced was, "What else could the seven-thousand square feet do on the other six days of the week"?

By then, I had been serving for some time on the elected leadership team of the Spokane Homeless Coalition. I knew numerous Spokane ministries and non-profits were doing an outstanding job of feeding the hungry, housing the homeless and getting medical and mental health treatment to the poverty stricken in our area. I also knew the system had a gap.

Once someone cleared a drug and alcohol treatment program, got food stamps, and received housing help, by living in some tiny, downtown, slum apartment, the next step-up turned out to be too big of a leap. People in the system were unable to pull up to the next level because their resumes said, "Four years an addict, two years in prison, three years living on the street." In a town where one hundred applications are filled out, just to flip burgers, it was too hard to get meaningful employment without skills and a past track record like that.

Rather than feed 175 people each week, hoping to really change the lives of ten to fifteen of them, we thought that we might move to the other end of the funnel and put more energy into the few and let Union Gospel Mission, Catholic Charities, and others handle the large meal programs. We thought that our best route would be to create a job training program with our church square footage but still allow us to do services on Sunday and other times. Sports fields, coffee shops, and pubs are the societal hubs our society gathers around today.

After kicking around what we could do with seven thousand square feet, we decided to build an open-to-the-public job-training café that mentored people out of poverty culture. We would open it all week long and then close it on Sundays to do church in the same space.

We planned on taking former inmates, addicts, or street people and give them jobs for training in the hard skills of work knowledge, and the soft skills of people interaction. We knew that many people growing up in poverty culture need to learn all the unspoken middle-class rules before they will ever fit in or find success.

We dreamed of building a café with enough meeting space that we could simultaneously hold Bible studies, youth gatherings, or recovery ministries, while the neighborhood met to commune at their favorite local coffee shop.

I wanted to hold regular Wednesday Night Wisdom talks at our coffee shop, where I used my connections and partnerships to create discussion nights where I could interview leaders and frontline practitioners who are doing outstanding work among the poor and marginalized, but they do not have a platform to communicate to the general public all that their work entails. I knew leaders running successful ministries with homeless women and kids, or men, who had been incarcerated and were trying to rebuild their lives. Still others did outstanding work with runaway teens and sex-trafficking rescue.

I thought it would be fantastic to have a church space where the whole city could come and listen and learn about all the tremendous government programs and non-profits that were literally changing the social structure of society with their efforts. Maybe with a little work, we could make Wednesday Night Wisdom talks a local cable access show.

We had four months to inspire our remaining church members with this vision, before the sale was completed.

44. RUMBLINGS ON SEATTLE FAULT LINES

We knew the money from the sale was going to be large, but the people-power was the same small group of diligent helpers who had always been in the struggle. If any of them dropped out and jumped ship, it wasn't going to work to leave only some of us rowing the boat. Right away, we decided that a couple of our board members would set up private meetings with each member of our church to hold discussions about the personal cost of making this leap. We weren't sure we could do it even if everyone agreed to stay on.

Some people would have emotional connections to the old site and weren't ever going to move. Their age and station of life was not meant for a change of this magnitude. Others were of the poverty class themselves and, realistically, had little to offer in skills or finances to assist us on the journey. Our selected board members met with each member to get feedback and hear their personal opinions, doubts and fears. We asked each member to sign one-year pledges if they were *all in*. The pledge was that for one year they would be willing to serve and give, come hell or high water, to make this transformation. After that, they would be free to leave with our blessing and find another church, if they wanted to go. We wanted to stress to them that if we aren't all going to do this journey then we aren't strong enough and we would be better off to quit now, and never undertake the project rather than have several of them abandon us during the escape plan. All but two of our non-elderly members agreed.

After we signed the papers to complete the sale of the building, before finding a new site, and long before we swung the first hammer to start construction, several of them who had signed the pledge, left us anyway. That's church people.

At the same time, board members where conducting those talks, we were also adjusting the board by electing new leadership because the requirements for the next phase of our journey would need some new talent and skills at the top levels; the time demands were going to increase.

A couple of us were tasked with traveling all over town, scouting potential new locations for the church. We looked at dozens of buildings in a wide range of area. We finally settled on a fantastic little corner store that sits on a main drag in an old 1940s era business district in the center of Spokane. It was a beer, cigarettes, and candy bar store, only a ten-minute drive north of downtown.

Our leaders all toured it and we took some of our people who have high gifts of spiritual discernment to the site. After praying over it, they all agreed this was where Jesus wanted us to move. It was 6,300 square feet on a main floor with 3,500 square feet of unfinished basement. It was also $80,000 cheaper than any other place we had investigated.

The plan was for the sale to close in early February 2014. We would be building out the new space, moving, hopefully open by May. We began collecting bids from contractors.

In January, Mars Hill leadership informed us that they were consolidating all of their holdings into one bank and wanted us to hold off on the closing date because our title, in limbo, would mess up their banking plan. Instead, they wanted us to roll the closing date to early April. We discussed it and agreed this would be fine. This was easier on us anyway.

We had a 12,000 square-foot building downtown, full of junk accumulated over one hundred years; the inventory and cleaning weren't going to be easy. We altered our plans to do our build-out through the summer months and reopen in September. Mars Hill had put down $30,000 in earnest money in November, so we asked for another $30,000. They agreed, and we adjusted the closing date to April.

In March of 2014, rumblings began regarding the entire structure of Mars Hill Church and its leader Mark Driscoll. Former staff members and lay volunteers began speaking out against the tyrannical practices of the pastor. Bloggers began to make it their personal mission to expose the church for being corrupt and abusive. Financial mismanagement accusations were being slung at them. I understood that, behind the scenes, Mars Hill was compiling a huge amount of money in a fund to deal with potential lawsuits and to possibly make restitution to former employees who had been unjustly dismissed. The stink of dead and rotting things was being dug up in Seattle, and we found ourselves downwind in Spokane.

A day before the April closing date, their financial officer called us to drop the bombshell that the lending institution with whom they had been consolidating all their financial holdings denied them any more loan money to purchase us. We could tell by their tone and bewildering shock that this was a momentous occasion. They had never been denied before in their history of big decisions. They were stunned, to say the least.

As I understood it, the previous October they had offered us just over $1.255 million for our site. At the same time, they offered $1.5 million for the vacant lot just to the south of us, and had another million to help get the Spokane satellite location up and running. Their plan was to put $375,000 down on our site and pay the rest through a loan. By the April closing date, they had only put down $60,000 in earnest money and they were broke. Their enterprises were disintegrating, giving was plummeting, and people were fleeing their churches like wildlife running from a forest fire.

They begged us for another thirty days. What choice did we have? We asked for another $30,000 in earnest money but they balked, claiming the financial officer didn't have authority to approve it. They couldn't do anything more. Our church treasurer, Bill, had spent his career in investment banking with Stanley Morgan. He began coaching their guy on what to do next and how to shop their loan around. They seemed to be inexperienced with getting a "no" answer and didn't know what to do next. We took a deep breath and waited while their world unraveled, shrunk, and twisted like cheap clothing in an unbalanced washing machine.

The deadline in May came and went, and we did not hear anything. We contacted them, only to find that some of the men who had been speaking with us were "no longer with the company." The main contact person who was the party responsible for the negotiation was "on vacation." I thought going on vacation with a million-dollar deadline on the table was a sign of belligerent lying—or gross incompetence.

I began to pack my office. We were not going to make the sale after all and the only alternative would be to simply close down. It was now the third or fourth time in my years as pastor that I was once again preparing to close a church. I expected to be gone before the end of summer.

A week later, they called us back to say they thought that we could carry the loan for them, and they were waiting for us to make terms to them. We had a denominational expert from our headquarters in Chicago who was helping us with all the real estate transactions and running the contracts past lawyers to help us out. They somehow got the idea from a loose conversation with him that we as a local church could carry the loan to them on our building. There was one main problem with that idea: we would have no money to go pursue *our* dream.

"No," we firmly responded. "This is *your* offer and *your* deal and at this point you need to make an offer on what you're purposing as the buyer. *Our* proposal is that you pay us the money you agreed to pay in the original offer or simply forfeit the earnest money, walk away, and we will resell to someone else." We realized we would have $60,000 to use while we put the building back up for sale. That might buy us a few extra months.

They came back with a proposal to put no additional money down and make $10,000 per month payments, all going to principle, for the next five years, and they would pay the balance at the end of that term.

"Let me get this straight," I answered our real estate agent on the phone when he informed me of their offer; "fifteen-thousand member, seventeen campus, $35 million in assets, and $30 million per year Mars Hill Church wants our thirty member, twenty drunks, and four dogs church that's $180,000 in debt, and loses $5,000 a month in income to take a five percent down payment, which we already own as forfeited earnest money, and then give them an *interest free loan* for over a *million bucks* over the next five years? You tell them, not only I said NO but…"

After a few more words and phrases which I thought Mark Driscoll would be very familiar with, from his own mouth, our real estate agent laughed and said, "Why don't you let me do the negotiating?"

Several days later, they came back with a deal which was to put no additional money down and pay interest only for five years on $1.255 million-dollar loan, which we would carry. So, they went from offering $10,000 a month to offering only $5,000 a month. I didn't even bother to respond to our agent—it was over—again.

I walked out of church on Sunday, May 11th, 2014, Mother's Day, knowing my years of effort had ended. We didn't have a sale, after all. We were out of money, out of time, and could not keep going. Jesus must have other plans. Six and one-half years of my ministry life seemed wasted, tossed aside. My wife and I began preparing to shut down the church and hand over the building keys to the denominational offices in Seattle. We planned on being out by the end of June.

Two weeks later, Mars Hill contacted us and offered to put an additional $190,000 down combining with their earnest money to make a $250,000 down payment on the agreed upon price of $1,255,000. They also agreed to make $10,000 a month payments for the next two years with half going to principle and half going to rent with a full purchase price of the balance (some $900,000) to be given at the end of the two years.

We contacted our beer, cigarettes, and candy bar grocery store owner, to see if we could swing the same deal with him. $65,000 down, $4,000 per month payments with half going to rent and half to principle and the balance paid, when our building sold in two years. He agreed. This meant we would have only $160,000 after paying real estate fees to do our build-out. It was super tight—but possible.

We inked the deal in June and prepared to move out in August. Our plan was to hold "volunteer work projects" on Sunday mornings, for the next three months. That meant we met at the new site, sing some worship music to lone acoustic guitar, and have a sermonette. The benediction to the service was usually something like, "Okay, everyone, put on your gloves, grab your hammers and crowbars, we're going to tear down this ceiling. AMEN!"

That would be church for the next few months. It would take more than three months to actually get it done. In the Fall 2014, well under way with our demolition, Mars Hill Pastor Mark Driscoll resigned; the church collapsed and broke apart. Mars Hill ceased to exist as an incorporated church by December. We were still under construction.

45. DYING ON THE TABLE

We all hear stories about people who undergo major and risky operations to save their lives. Sometimes these are so risky the outcomes are not in their favor to survive. In some cases, the crash happens during surgery and more than one story is told about a person dying on the table while undergoing the risky procedure. The miracle is that they survive anyway.

Once we had nailed down our new location we had to get contractor bids to see if a build-out was even feasible, for the $160,000 we had left, before we inked a deal to buy. Several contractors pitched ideas and plans way out of our price range. One gave us a time and materials bid that fit our ideas providing there were no major surprises, and, that much of the work could be done by our teams of volunteers at key points in the build-out. The risk was high. Something always goes wrong in construction. It's not what we wanted to do but the alternative was just to roll over and die. We saw it as a risky, life-saving surgery. Escape plans out of zombie land are never easy.

For many weeks, our services consisted of showing up at the new site and holding our simple devotional service, then tearing down walls and ceilings for hours afterward. Many times, some of the nonphysical workers provided lunch for the team. We laughed, played, and had a great time among all the dirt and sweat. It wasn't so bad until we had to tear out the restrooms and went to a single outhouse. Our plan was only to endure such suffering, until early November when we would have new restrooms online. Little did we know that our single outhouse would serve us through the winter, clear past the New Year.

In any remodel of this magnitude the more you pull down the more you see. Sometimes it meant major changes in plumbing or electric plans. Sometimes it resulted in esthetic issues. The existing ceiling was a double height affair with long rows of institutional fluorescent light banks that produced flickering, headache-inducing light. Our plan was to raise the lower portions of the ceiling, which were eight feet tall, to the eleven-foot height of the main ceiling area. Once we began to demo things, we realized there was ceiling above the upper ceiling. It was as if someone put in a low ceiling in the 1970's underneath the original 1941 ceiling. We peaked through both layers and found this outstanding shiplap, tongue and groove wooden ceiling with these incredible black iron crossbeams as the original construction. The decision was immediately made to tear out the entire ceiling over the main area, exposing the fantastic architectural feature. This raised the ceiling height to thirteen feet and gave us built-in trusses for stage lighting.

We then had to consider issues of insulation which were in flux anyway. We knew the existing roof was in rough shape but our original thoughts, and the bid proposal, was to simply patch it for a cost of around $6,000. The roof turned out to be far worse than anticipated and had to be replaced, but this meant we could insulate the entire building with a new roof, adding more to the cost but saving thousands in interior changes. The new insulated roof cost $40,000. Our plans meant that any huge change like that resulted in cuts elsewhere. We had to scale back lighting, restroom ideas, and dump our kitchen equipment plans immediately. We pressed on with a scaled down version of our ideas, but it was still going to work, and the overall designs were going to be pretty cool.

One day, our Homeless Coalition meeting had a candidate's forum prior to an election. State representatives and senators came to discuss issues pertaining to the Coalition and homeless advocacy. I introduced myself to one of our two local representatives, Marcus Riccelli. He came up to see our under-construction site, get a tour, and hear about our vision.

"What do you need from me?" He asked in a tone that hinted he was eager to help.

I answered, in a casual way, like I was asking for bus fare to get downtown, "I need you to help me access grants, to get about $15,000 in kitchen equipment."

"Okay," he said, just as casually as a guy reaching into his pocket for spare change. "Each representative has access to some discretionary funds for our districts, for projects just like this. "I can get that for you."

I was stunned!

A few days later I filled out a couple pages for a grant application and sent it back. The next session of the state representatives approved it; they sent us another twenty pages of documents and verification paperwork to fill out. It was a reimbursement grant. We had to raise the money first but at least this grant was there to access when the time came to buy kitchen equipment.

About two-thirds of the way into construction, things began to slow way down. In late October, I would come to my little, outdoor, portable office-shed (like one sees on construction sites) and I realized no one was on the work site that day. Crews came only once or twice a week after that and, by the first week of November, no one showed up anymore. We were nowhere close to being finished.

My calls were not returned. Many of the guys on the plumbing, electric, and carpentry side had started donating hours of work, just to try and help get us done. But the end zone was simply too far away, to keep running down the field and getting hit. I knew that we were out of money, but our contractor was reticent to tell us. He had spent several weeks trying to get crews to donate time to us. He had succeeded as long as possible. We weren't built-out enough to get anywhere close to opening. We were flat lined, dead on the table. *Beeeeeeeeeeeep.*

We needed a new floor, the restrooms weren't completed, wires still hung from areas around the building, and walls weren't textured or painted. We were thousands of dollars away from finishing. The thing we dreaded most, having surprises, had happened—too often. We set up a meeting just after Thanksgiving to discuss the bad news.

I admit, I was mad that we weren't told when we were down to the last $10,000, or so. I would have told the contractor to stop everything and just finish the lady's restroom if nothing else got done. We had a single outhouse for four months during the winter cold and snow. My wife and daughters had taken to going to the bathroom at home before getting in the car to go to church.

"Time for church," the call would go out, only to hear the patter of feet rush to the restrooms, even if they didn't have to go. None of my girls wanted to get caught at church needing to use the outhouse. I'm sure several other ladies did the same. But still, they came. Still, they sang. Still, they prayed. Still, they worked.

I walked through the abandoned, cold, and empty site, every day, in the middle of November. The silence was deafening, after all those weeks of construction sounds. I prayed, a lot. I knew we were broke but I hadn't been officially told. Under these conditions, there was no way we could open and get an occupancy permit. The work needed to get the restrooms and electric work done were huge in themselves, let alone everything else that was needed. After all the risk and years of hardship on behalf of this church and its ministries, I felt more than a little cheated.

Discouragement is too soft a word to explain my feelings. Anxiety and tension were a constant state of being. My daily prayers were like, "Hey God, if you knew this was going to be the result then we shouldn't have even started; we now have an unusable and unsellable building; we don't know what to do, and we don't know how to solve this." I was at the end of all my answers. "You'd better do something, because we sure can't do anything. We're out of effort and out of ideas."

It was a tough Thanksgiving week. Two days before our meeting with the contractor, at which we knew he planned to tell us that we were hopelessly broke, a $20,000 surprise check came in the mail. Again, it turned out that a very old Covenant member, who forgot to change her will as she left angry many years before, incidentally (or by God's perfect design) left us a, nice-sized, chunk money. We were the beneficiaries of her negligence. The woman had died almost a year before, and after a lot of probate and court arguments, the dust settled, and we were the recipients of that $20,000. We had no idea about any of this. It wasn't enough to finish the job but, like a relay race, the baton was being passed, for at least running the next distance. We picked it up, and we ran.

While we turned the contractor loose on finishing the women's restroom as cheap as possible, a bunch of guys in the church set out putting down a new floor. We worked through the

Christmas break with our teachers, students, and anyone who could take a day off while we laid subflooring down. Next, we got a super sweet deal from a professional floorer, to lay the tile. We advanced one more level, after being totally dead. It wasn't enough to get across the finish line, but we sure were closer.

Fourteen months earlier, when we first received the offer to sell, we had planned on opening in September 2014. We were, at that point, about five months behind. We began to pray for a way to open by Easter 2015. We went through the $20,000 quickly and found ourselves broke and dead on the table again, just after the New Year. We were still far from being finished.

In my associations with Coalition members, I had met many leaders in various non-profit agencies, who work with the poor. Many of them were aware of our plans to turn the church square footage into a job training coffee shop during the week for poverty culture people, and former addicts and convicts. They loved the idea and thought more churches should think that creatively.

The guy who was the Mormon Church's head person for organizing all the various members in Spokane County to do community outreach works dropped by one day. He was a friend of mine, from all the meetings we had sat in together.

"Wow this place is cool," he exclaimed as he walked through, one cold day in early January. "When are you going to get finished and open?"

"Um, that's a funny story..." I began. I told him of our economic situation.

"I used to own a painting business," he informed me. "How about if I could get a crew down here to paint the base coat of everything in one day? Do you think you could afford the paint? It would be about $600."

"Yes, I could swing that," I answered enthusiastically. We picked a day for him to come down.

"By the way, if you could prepare the outside of the building for us, we will come down when the weather gets warm in March and paint that too." So, the Mormons painted us, for free.

A new economics professor at Whitworth University, which is a Presbyterian school, was a friend of mine and she contacted me a few days later. "Do you think your church would have a work project that our business club could fulfill?" She asked. "And if you could take about half an hour to share the vision of the church, at the time, that would be great." She added.

We had the University Business Club prepare the outside of the building by taking down signs, scraping old paint, and fixing some exterior problems. The Mormons painted us, at zero-cost, inside and out. We saved about $15,000 on that one. Presbyterians and Mormons combined to help build an Evangelical Covenant Church. We were flatlined again—but it wasn't over yet.

Our downtown location was right next-door to a drug addiction recovery facility, run by a local church called The Dream Center (not affiliated with a famous one, with the same name, in Los Angeles). They needed some work projects for their forty, or more, men. We proposed a deal with them; every Tuesday and Thursday, thirty to forty guys, in various stages of recovery, arrived and did all the interior detail painting for only the cost of cheeseburgers, which we bought across the street from our new place. So, Mormons *and* drug addicts painted us, for no-cost labor. We just paid for paint and cheeseburgers.

Late January 2015, I happened to have a meeting with Rob McCann the head of Catholic Charities (for the entire Eastern side of Washington State). After our meeting, he asked how things were going in our buildout. I offered to show him, so we drove up to the site.

Catholic Charities builds multi-million-dollar housing complexes and homeless shelters in our town, among the many other things they do for the poor. He walked our site and was simply stunned at how much we had accomplished and how far we had come on only $160,000.

"This is actually amazing!" He said with awe and wonder. "This could easily be a half million-dollar project." I was simultaneously pleased that we had done so well yet embarrassed that we were so blatantly ignorant, when we entered the project. After a long pause, while looking around, he added, "How much do you need to finish and open?"

I let out one of those exasperated, defeated sighs and said disgustedly, "We're probably $75,000 short."

"I think I can get you that." He said, as cheerfully as if he was offering to buy lunch.

It turns out that, concerning their grants and loans for buildings, the organization can't pocket any leftovers from grants received. Any money left must go towards another charity doing similar work for the poverty culture. Our café counted.

We got a $50,000 grant from the Catholics to help finish, by my completion of some simple paperwork. That huge amount took us almost to the end, but we were still going to fall short by about $20,000. This was going to be the third time we crashed on the table, under construction, before opening.

When Mars Hill fell apart they decided to close all their churches that had no chance of individual survival. They sold several properties, paid off debts, and redistributed money to the dozen, or so, surviving satellite campuses, which then became independent churches.

The little group of one hundred people who were going to plant the Mars Hill campus in our old building downtown felt very strongly that they had an excellent chance to keep going. They changed their name to Redemption Church and became independent.

One of the sites they sold was the main flagship building in Ballard, a neighboring area of Seattle. A sister church in our denomination, Quest Church, was negotiating the deal to purchase it. The same guy, Rollie Persson, from our Chicago headquarters (who had negotiated our sale) was negating that deal. A year or so later, I would learn from Rollie that Mars Hill had been discussing simply dumping the remainder of our contract and walking away. Because the sale of the Ballard campus was several million dollars, he implicated that they had to do right by us in Spokane—or no sale would happen in Seattle.

In late February, Mars Hill informed us that they would pay off their debt for the remaining $5,000 per month that they owed on the principle. This amounted to a $75,000 payout. They would also give enough cash to Redemption Church in Spokane to cover the other $5,00 in rent payments for the next year and half. This unexpected cash payout put us over the top. It was the final electric zap bringing us back to life.

Had Mars Hill not crashed we never would have received that sum, at that time, and we probably would not have opened. Redemption Church had to agree that by May 2016 the final pay-off balance, around $900,000, would be satisfied. If they couldn't pay it, we would be forced to repossess the downtown building. But that was more than a year away. With this $75,000, we were put over the top of our budget requirement for completion. Mars Hill's death meant we would live.

We hustled throughout February and March, to finish everything we needed. Easter week we were still scrambling. We held an open house to show off the site on the Wednesday night before Easter. We served lots of coffee drinks that night. Two hundred people came by to support us.

On Good Friday, we still needed our occupancy permit to open. The offices in the planning department closed at noon. At 11:00am, we were just able to run down there with paperwork to finish it all. We still needed two more inspections. The secretary there put out an email that asked if any of their inspectors would volunteer to help us out. She actually used the phrase "Let's give them an Easter Miracle," in her email. Several inspectors showed up and cleared us. We got our occupancy permit on Good Friday, right at closing hours.

After 127 years of existence, we held our first service on Easter Sunday 2015 in our new location. 141 people showed up, including some Mormons and some Catholics. Moreover, I didn't see any dogs in church that day.

46. CHURCH IS A DIRTY WORD

When we were building out the space and designing a coffee shop, we kept talking about how to manage it and run it and what the best method and structure for leadership should be like trying to do both church and café. We had two huge concerns. One was that we really didn't want our church board to sit around discussing economic issues about coffee shop business. We didn't want to bog them down meetings with agenda items containing the wholesale prices of bagels and pounds of coffee beans. We wanted our church leaders to focus their efforts and energies dealing with spiritual issues and church productivity concerns.

The second concern was about funding. We had learned years before that the word, "church," in a name, prevents businesses, government agencies, and some foundations from donating to a worthy cause. They may love what you do and want to give, but company and corporate policies forbid giving to churches, so they simply can't and won't write a check that includes the word, "church," –in any form. Our limited funds were all going to the build out of the site, but our job training coffee shop was now going to need a lot of additional funding to get up and running and that meant getting bigger donations.

For five years, we had run the downtown free Sunday afternoon meal to the street people. During that time, we had learned a lot about raising funds. We had hit the "no church" policy, many times over, with companies and foundations whom otherwise would have cheerfully granted us financial help.

We had been running the meals under a church account that we simply separated out like a mission's budget item. Donations to the church were sorted as designated giving to the meal program, which we called Street Wise, or to the general fund, depending on the donor's request. Since all the checks coming in had to be made out to the church, it caused us a lot of headaches, many times over. Helpful office volunteers ended up opening the mail and putting checks in all the wrong places. Since my wife ran Street Wise, and she and our bookkeeper were the only ones who knew which names were church givers and which donations were raised by Street Wise efforts, they had to take over sorting the mail.

Of course, in the church world no one understands the myriads of problems previously caused by not distinguishing these donations, church people just see the pastor's wife as an over-controlling hag because she won't let anyone else open the mail;

poor, diligent pastors' wives. About two years into doing the meals we finally filed to create a separate *501c3* for Street Wise, so that we could easily receive business donations.

More than two years after filing, we had quit doing the meals, had packed everything up, and moved out of the downtown location. In the Fall 2014, I was sitting in my portable office trailer, which was now parked outside the building where we were deep into our construction plan. One day, I opened a letter from the IRS, announcing they had granted our *501c3* non-profit status for Street Wise, and they were making it retroactive to April 2011, when we first applied. I laughed out loud. It took the IRS more than three years to grant it. They must have known we were conservatives, even if we weren't a tea party.

"Hey Jesus, thanks but you're a couple of years too late on this one. We aren't even doing the meals anymore!" And I kept laughing. But then... "Hey wait a minute," I thought to myself; or, the idea was planted... whatever, "This could be the answer to our coffee shop problem," I thought. "We could subcontract the operation of the coffee shop and the job training component to Street Wise, use the new *501c3* to raise corporate and foundation funding to launch it, and, we would have the added benefit that ex-cons and newly recovered addicts wouldn't technically be on church payroll or staff but would work for Street Wise."

The fact that I was the president of Street Wise and my wife was director of the new corporation would insure that the two entities of church and business would stay closely tied. The timing was just too weird for it not to be a sign from God that He had plans for Street Wise to keep going.

The church board liked the idea of subcontracting out the operation of the coffee shop to Street Wise. This meant the church would own the property and all the equipment, but the actual payroll of the trainees, the coffee and pastry costs, and sales would never cross into the church coffers. Food and labor costs to run the coffee shop would stay independent of the church books. Once the coffee shop was up, running, and producing an income, the profit would be split between Street Wise and the church. The plan was that the coffee shop would pay rent out of the profit margins. It took a little more time to get all the permits for that processed and set up the accounts for goods and inventory and all that goes with opening a café. The church opened the first Sunday in April and the coffee shop opened three weeks later.

We have come a long way from calling ourselves, "The Swedish Tabernacle." For another sixty years we had been "First Covenant," which I always thought sounded like a colonial, imperialistic name. I always pictured a big Swedish lumberjack in buckskins planting a denominational flag on a hill, claiming the land for king and denomination. Just before making this move, we voted to change our name. The sign on the front of the new building now read, "THE GATHERING HOUSE *a covenant church and café.*" That little word on the subtitle "church" kept people from entering.

For weeks, we would have people wander in look about and tentatively ask, "So, what is this place?"

"It's a coffee shop, six days a week. On Sundays we just close the coffee shop and hold church here. What can we get you today," our baristas would happily answer.

"I knew it was a church, so I thought you were only open on Sundays for coffee," would be one of the replies we would get.

"I've been driving by for months now and saw that you were open. I finally decided to come in and try it. It actually doesn't look like a church at all," some people would say to us, in a surprised fashion.

"My friend finally invited me to come in and promised you wouldn't preach at me if I got a coffee; hey, this place is pretty cool. I like what you've done," would be another type of response we heard.

We could always tell who was new because they would come in, stop in the entryway, and simply gaze around with wonder on their faces, taking in the décor, which is pretty impressive and makes us happy—that our hard work and designs are so greatly appreciated.

The new site was an art deco building. We researched 1941 colors and painted the building in shades of salmon, teal, tan, and deep blue. The colors were all picked off popular trends from that era. Besides, the theme fit exactly with the inspiring iron crossbeam trusses on the ceiling, the wonderful tongue and groove shiplap board; we even tore old plaster off some of the walls to reveal the original brick structure.

The old church downtown had solid oak twelve-foot long pews, which we couldn't give away for free. We found a woodworker who agreed to convert them into our coffee shop tables for a really good price. Our tables are two-inch thick, sixty-five-year-old, solid oak repurposed pews. The barista bar is the old church pulpit which we pulled out of the old building and brought with us. The flooring is a black and white checkered pattern, also mimicking the 1940s art deco period. We salvaged a section of ornate tin roof and original light fixtures, used in the back hallway. We custom built bathrooms to fit the look of the 1940s period. Our stage and sound booth were also built out of old pew wood. The shelves in my office and behind the barista bar are pew benches. All in all, people keep commenting on how much they love being here, how wonderful it is for the neighborhood, and how it is becoming their favorite hangout. But, it's taken them time to get over it being a church.

Two business leaders in the district pulled me aside on different occasions. One gave me a genuine apology for not supporting us sooner. She said she had spoken against us at business meetings when she heard we were moving into the neighborhood. She thought we were planning on bringing the street meal to her neighborhood. Once she understood we were going to be a middleclass, job-training program for people getting out of poverty life, she became our biggest supporter. The other leader was a real estate agent and property owner who owns a lot of the buildings in the business district.

He told me, "I was so angry when I heard a church bought the anchor tenant location because it is one of the most prime locations in the whole neighborhood." He was furious it was going to be used for just a lousy church site. "But now that I've seen what you guys really built," he would confide to me, "I think this is fantastic for the neighborhood and I'm really glad you're here." He is another of our biggest supporters.

We struggled with whether we should simply dump the subtitle with the word, "church," in it. But we didn't want to hide who we are. We didn't want to bait-and-switch people with any kind of manipulative trickery. We didn't want, ever, to be ashamed of our association with Jesus. But, it almost killed our coffee shop in the first six months. We lost a lot of money trying to keep the coffee shop afloat. On the other hand, because the word, "church," was on the building outside, the number one evangelism tool was the coffee shop.

"So, this is a church?" People would ask our baristas, several times a week. "What's the church like? What's it all about?" And many of them would try out a church service.

Our ex-con, ex-addict, poverty culture baristas would pitch our church to our customers and pass out church literature only when asked. By far the single biggest draw for Sunday morning services is from people who first come to our building to buy coffee during the week. People can feel that the place is different. Our church grows because of the coffee shop. Our coffee shop struggles because we're a church. It's still an unresolved dilemma.

47. BREATHING

I walked out of my office a while back to get a cup of coffee in our café. It had been just a little over a year since opening. I stood there a moment and surveyed the room. Eight ladies who manage the local Union Gospel Mission Women's Recovery Shelter were sitting around a couple of tables, discussing new plans and strategies for fresh ministry. Two other ladies in Salvation Army uniforms were enjoying coffees at another table, and seemed to be in a deep personal discussion. A young woman I knew as the Young Life leader at the high school (half a mile away) was talking with the head of Christ Kitchen, a restaurant style ministry that helps rescue women from homelessness or street life. Additionally, some men were in the front corner by the main windows holding a Bible study. Two Moody Bible students had their laptops open and were doing homework. None of these people attend our church services.

We had come a long way from being a downtown brick cathedral surrounded by poverty culture, addicts, and homeless street people. I was no longer sitting in a huge quiet, empty building all week long pretending that we could fill it on Sundays with an inspirational, attractive service. We no longer dealt with trying to overcome the neighborhood image; and, to be honest it smells nice in our church now when the congregation gathers. I still get amazed when I think that I had tried to close the church three times during my tenure. God, though, wouldn't let go of it. We were now doing church as a coffee shop—the center of a neighborhood. It's fun to come to work every day—I meet the most incredible people.

Jesus uses our café space, all the time, for His purposes. Quite a lot of ministry happens here that is not run by our church. I see Bible studies going on all the time. Sometimes our church attendance grows by people who have left their churches but kept their Bible studies. For lack of location they've moved their Bible studies here and, since they are currently "churchless," they try us out.

Almost every day some other pastor from another church is sitting there with Bibles, commentaries, and reference books open, doing studies or sermon preparation. It's not uncommon to have multiple pastors holding meetings, from all kinds of various churches, on any given day. Other times, it's leaders of Youth for Christ, Young Life, Family Promise, or numerous other Christian, non-profit agencies and para-church ministries. We seem to be one of the hubs for every new church planter coming to town. The network of pastors here has grown so tight that, on our second Easter, six of us churches in the neighborhood united to do one large combined Easter service in the local six hundred seat movie theater, just three blocks away. Each of us pastors took a slice of the service; it was a fantastic experience and an inspiring display of unity—all under the banner of Jesus and His Word.

The neighborhood and city often use our site, too. The local business district holds their meetings in our conference rooms.

We've held fund raisers for them and for agencies like Salvation Army, and still others. The city's neighborhood council has moved that meeting to our site, as well. Shortly after we opened, the mayor of Spokane held a conference in our site, with business leaders, discussing the impact of hiring people who were formerly incarcerated. One such former convict, Dave Dahl of Dave's Killer Bread, from Portland Oregon, was the featured speaker. He sold the bread business for $200 million a month later. The citywide Homeless Coalition has opted to move their one-hundred-member, sixty-agency, monthly meetings to The Gathering House. In fact, at the time I'm writing this, they had their meeting this morning and numerous state representative and senators were in our coffee-shop-church, to discuss statewide issues pertaining to homelessness, crime, poverty culture, and mental illness. City council members have come to our coffee shop as speakers or to hold workshops and meetings on issues of poverty in our city. Whenever I bump into the mayor in public settings he asks how our church and café are doing. We're a county of over 500,000 people. It amazes me that Jesus would put us on the mayor's radar.

We also became a cultural hub, serving as an art gallery for artists to display their works, along with art shows. A local African American jazz group and entertainment business uses us for open mic nights. A woman rents us on the first Friday of each month to have vintage lindy hop swing dance lessons with live music. We've done concerts and comedy shows. They aren't always Christian, but we have one rule: they must be family-friendly in content. Recovery people constantly tell us how nice it is to hear live music again, since they dropped out of the bar scene long ago to get healthy.

One day, a guy who was a regular in our coffee shop approached me. I knew him as a real estate agent and board member of one of the churches a few blocks away. He was also the chairman of a group called International Assistance Partners (IAP). They were a network of influential Christian businessmen and bankers who financed micro-business enterprise overseas. They had access to numerous business donation dollars that had to stay local because of certain laws and policies. They had been discussing that, if they couldn't get the money to the third world, then maybe they should focus on the third world, which had come to us. They started discussions with World Relief, the local Christian agency that resettles refugees in Spokane, along with another group, Spokane Neighborhood Action Partners (SNAP), which had received a federal grant for business training and development of refugees. The three agencies had been in talks for months about launching ethnic food restaurants for refugee families to create sustainable businesses. They had settled on starting off with a food truck to test market the menus and ideas. They were having trouble finding locations that suited the city, their business model, and the health department.

"Would you guys be interested in being the location?" He asked me.

"Sure" I answered "That fits our heartbeat. What do you need?"

"We need a fully operational, health department approved, industrial kitchen that we could rent out for fifteen dollars per hour, for about twenty hours per week. We need a fixed location to establish the food truck. The health department demands that we place it on pavement, not gravel, so one space in the back corner of your parking lot would be ideal, since it's a busy corner spot. We would like access to water and electricity too. We will need a greywater drain installed somewhere on site. We plan on paying rent for this, too."

"We don't actually have a full operational kitchen," I answered, sadly. "We had to cut out kitchen equipment and some of the mandatory kitchen upgrade when we ran out of money building the place. But, what if I can raise the money somehow? ...I do have access to a reimbursement grant from the state to pay for the kitchen equipment."

"What else does the kitchen need, besides that?"

"About $6,000 in health code upgrades." I answered, "New flooring, sink improvements, and such. We'll have to raise that, too."

"No problem. International Assistance Partners will give you a grant for $6,000 and then we will front you the $15,000 to buy the equipment and you can pay it back, after you submit the receipts to the state for reimbursement."

Just like that, we built our kitchen and launched an ethnic food truck with a refugee from Afghanistan. They had fantastic kabobs. The food truck provided a generous monthly income and our new kitchen enabled us to expand our coffee shop to a full-scale restaurant. We serve killer gourmet grilled cheese sandwiches, stellar soup, and an outstanding salad bar.

This was an outstanding move for us, on two fronts. First, barista work requires a pretty high functioning awareness with multi-tasking abilities. We had to let some of our trainees go, in the past year, who simply couldn't keep up. Had we the ability to offer focused kitchen skill training, we could have kept them. Second, the income generated solely from the resale of baked goods and espresso was not enough to sustain the whole enterprise, especially with the handicap of "church" on the exterior sign.

It was for all these economic enterprises, events, and artistic expressions that we decided to *not* opt-out on paying the property taxes as a church. Once a church opts-out of property taxes, all these enterprises, meetings, art shows, and concerts become off limits. The kind of church we do now is way too fun to lose all that.

For five years, we held a Sunday afternoon, free community meal. 150-200 people came, each week, to eat the only free hot meal served downtown on Sundays. We would watch football or NASCAR together and then give out hygiene packs, hats, gloves, shoes, or coats. We made a lot of street friends. It was wild and sometimes crazy. Once in a while, the cops or medical emergency units were called, but we built a great reputation with the street culture as well as the city government.

Everyone said, "That's what the church should be doing! Good for you guys, more churches should do that!" But of course, they wouldn't come. They wouldn't attend. They wouldn't volunteer or give to keep it going.

Sunday church services had been down to thirty members, twenty street people and four dogs. About thirty of us stayed through the build-out. Now we have about 140 people attending on a regular basis (each Sunday) and we're growing. We no longer have board meetings where the topic on the agenda is, "How drunk can someone be and still attend services?" Or, "Where do we put the shopping carts full of personal belongings during the services to keep the safe?" The church giving can now pay the bills, which was quite a change following six years of monthly losses. For seven years while I pastored this church, we lost money every month; sometimes the losses were to the tune of $5,000 per month, yet we were still standing. We were an economic miracle of improbability.

We are no longer sitting in twelve thousand square feet of building on a downtown corner site that our church occupied since 1905. We had known what it was like to have forty thousand cars per day drive by us—and not know our name. Almost everyone I meet around town has heard of The Gathering House—even if they can't figure out what we are.

We had one last hurdle. On May 31, 2016 the little start-up church that was once a Mars Hill satellite campus, but was now and independent church plant, would owe us about $900,000. We would have to repossess the building, if they couldn't' come up with the money. Worse than that, we owed about $300,000 on our new location, due on the same date, or else the previous owner could repossess our site. We had no doubt that he would do that, in a heartbeat, after all the improvements we made. We also had no doubt that the congregation downtown would be unable to come up with such a huge sum after being in business for less than two years. They too, were about 150 people on a Sunday.

In March of that year, their pastor and I met for coffee. He said that although their people were deeply committed, and income was round $20,000 per month, no bank would give them a loan because they hadn't been in business long enough. They were out of options. God had been doing some odd things on this journey so far, so this time I didn't panic or anything. I'm not sure I had the energy to panic left in me. We just prayed.

Quietly, behind the scenes, I began talking to some wealthy California friends about buying our site for us and becoming our landlords. If we could hold on to this site, we could repossess the old site, re-sell it, and pay off the mortgage to the new investor—if push came to shove. It would take several months but that seemed to be our only hope. By mid-April I had pledges of only about $175,000 to buy our building. Nothing is ever easy. It's a funny feeling to be rich on paper but broke in daily operations, all the time.

Many years ago, when I planted a church I went looking for a denomination to join. That's how I found the Evangelical Covenant in the first place. A great denomination has resources of intelligence and skills to offer at crucial times. They have finances too, if they are exceptional, albeit the latter always come with strings attached. At the end of April, six weeks before the deadline, our denomination which was very aware of our situation came up with an incredible idea. The loaning branch called National Covenant Properties (NCP) was forbidden (by policy) to loan to churches that were not part of our denomination. They planned to give us the $900,000. We would then loan it to the start-up church that bought our old site for something like six-percent interest. They would pay it back to us to cover their debt obligation. We then would pay off the $300,000 or so balance of our mortgage and pay off the $180,000 equity line of credit we still owed NCP, which had been used the previous four years to keep us alive. We would then pass the loan to our (Covenant) conference office in Seattle, so that we would not be stuck as a lending institution. NCP would earn the sic-percent and the Pacific Northwest Conference office would hold the deed on the old site while awaiting a payoff when Redemption church would finally secure a bank loan in a couple of years.

The one caveat was that, once this deal was done, neither the conference office nor NCP had any additional funds to place in reserve, to cover, if Redemption Church ended up defaulting and being unable to come up with a loan. About $100,000 was needed to place in reserves until the debt was paid in full. The entity that did have those kinds of funds was... *Us*! In fact, we would have more than enough left over. We became an economic powerhouse after being on the bottom of the flow chart for all these years!

My super-intelligent church board members countered that if we were the ones securing the loan, so to speak, we would retain a percentage of the property rights if it did default. I make this sound so easy but, in fact, the conversations were a bit dicey, at least until all the dust settled and everyone knew where we stood. We closed the deal, handled all the exchanges, and for the first time in over seven years, we could financially breathe. The air feels good. I like breathing.

48. I CAN'T TALK ABOUT IT

I would love to leave you with the impression that we were just so creative, insightful, and full of courage that God rewarded us for being really special people. That wouldn't be true. I'd like to tell you that we simply walked into a desperate situation and knew exactly what to do and we had all the right skills, talents and knowledge to mobilize a dead congregation back to life. That would make us seem pretty hot! But it would be a false story. We were hopeless, scared, ignorant, broken and ill-equipped to do anything much at all.

The ten, or so, of us who are still standing from that very harsh beginning can pinpoint the actual day when things shifted and changed. It was Sunday, September 9th, 2009. We had just made it through a catastrophic conflict in which a group of people wanted to oust the senior pastor and kick him out. This was less than ten months after agreeing to sell him and his wife the parsonage to bring money into the coffers, to hire him some help to revitalize. *I* was that help.

The vote had been tallied and, after the dust settled, the church, instead, agreed to keep him on in a supporting role and I became the lead pastor. We gave him a few weeks off to regroup his thoughts and plan for a different future. At the time, we didn't know it, but he would resign in less than sixty days. Because of his new duties we had to lay off three support staff members who were contributing almost nothing to our survival anyway. We had been losing $15,000 per month, all year long, and these changes cut those losses down to only $5,000 per month. In this process, the church leadership board, which had proved grossly dysfunctional, had been asked to resign in mass; we were in a lull preparing to elect a new board. I had officially become the senior leader of the church, just five days earlier. My first Sunday as senior pastor, I couldn't talk.

I got one of those late summer colds and it had settled into my lungs and throat. I woke up that Sunday barely able to whisper. I was slated to sing and preach just like I would do for next several years. The other pastor was out of town with his wife. On the way to church that morning my two teenage daughters told me they could easily cover the singing if I just played guitar.

"But what will you do for the message"? They asked, with some trepidation. I made some gestures that either of them could step up and preach.

"Fat chance" They both laughed.

"That would be the shortest sermon ever."

I thought for a moment and decided that God must have timed this out for a reason. I'm the kind of guy who will push through almost anything and the only way to take me down is to take me out. I could walk and play but I could barely talk. We didn't have any back up people, of any caliber, who could cover for me. It dawned on me that maybe talk wasn't needed. God wanted something else that day, something unusual.

When the time came for a message I stepped up to the microphone and with all I had in me I pushed out the words as hard as I could. I sounded like someone strangling a seal.

"I... can't... talk... today," I began, barely above a whisper that the microphone could hardly pick up.

"I... think... God... wants us... to pray... but not in here.... and not... for each other." I looked around the room with little expectation of success. I drew a deep breath, to continue.

"So, what we're... going to do is... take the time... we would normally... sit here... for a sermon... and instead... walk outside the building... and ask anyone we meet... if we could... pray for them."

I was thinking inside that there was little chance of anyone actually doing this, but I could sense the Holy Spirit compelling me to offer the chance, even though I thought He was about to be sorely disappointed.

"When you're done...", My barking seal voice now felt and sounded more like a dying walrus, "come back in here . . . and let's share . . . what God does." I finished, exhausted.

I set down my guitar and sat. The church was still and silent. No one talked or coughed or moved. Then, ever so slowly, a couple of people got up and began to shuffle toward the doors. Like a steady stream, everyone started to rise and move outside, still being silent. In a few moments, there was just myself, a couple of infirmed elderly ladies, and one physically handicapped person in the room. All of them had their heads bowed in silent prayer.

I was completely taken off guard because I had expected maybe ten people to do this while another forty, or so, sat in either stubborn silence or mundane chit-chat. But, they had all moved outside. The place stayed empty and silent for about a half-hour.

Then, just as slowly, people began to return. Only they returned with lightness in their step and radiant faces. They were laughing or beaming from ear to ear. I could sense their joy, which was highly unusual for this particular gathering of people. A few of them were bringing in guests whom they had just met outside. One of my daughters had a homeless family of a young couple with three kids in tow. She had found them standing in a sandwich line a few blocks away.

"Does anyone... want to share... what you just experienced?" I hoarsely spoke over the microphone to those coming back in. They began to line up to speak.

One woman shared how she went to the Starbucks across the street and explained to a couple of young ladies that the pastor in the building beside them was too hoarse to preach, so they had come out to pray for people instead of listening to a sermon. She asked if there was anything she could pray for them.

"Sure," they eagerly replied; they were local college students studying for a test that they, reportedly, did not have any confidence in their abilities to pass. She prayed for them; they gave her a hug, afterward, when thanking her.

One woman walked up to the burger joint a block or two south of us and met a lady cop who wanted prayer for protection and wisdom to face her day.

Others met men lying in the allies behind our businesses and prayed for physical ailments or specific things they needed. Some of them asked prayer for family members they lost touch with but still remembered in their hearts and minds.

The sharing went on for a long time. No one met anyone that morning who turned down prayer. Everyone had a powerful encounter with the Holy Spirit as they prayed for strangers and talked with them. It was a spiritual awakening for many of our church people.

An elderly couple told me that they had never really seen the people around their church before. They were amazed at how much poverty and brokenness was literally lying outside their doorsteps. I was dumbfounded that they were just now acquiring this knowledge of their own neighborhood. But the truth is they live miles away and only came to this part of town for church. Their focus on the church was so strong that they had honestly never seen what was all around them.

Prior to my coming, I was told that the church used to throw a lavish Thanksgiving meal every year—*for themselves*! I was aghast when I heard that. They thought they were building community among the church with their efforts; I was shocked by their obtuseness. They weren't evil people. They were simply blind.

The young couple with three little kids was living out of a car. They were trying to get their lives together but no shelters at that time in Spokane would take whole families. In those days men went to one shelter and women and kids to another; it was tough to reunite, afterward. They gave a testimony about how drug addiction had caused them to lose everything. They were out of funds, out of food, and out of ideas. We would put them up in a hotel for several days and help them get settled. They would stay with us for several weeks. I would end up marrying the couple that was only living together with their three children. Some weeks later, they moved on and I never heard from them or saw them again—until I was writing this chapter.

Nine years to the day that they had walked into our church, a little note popped up on our Facebook page from them: "Pastor Rob married my wife, Casey and I. Helped us out of a dark spot in our lives. Grateful and Thankful."

I sent him a message through the links there and found out that he and his wife were still together and doing well. A local pastor's wife took their three kids to church every Sunday, but they didn't go much themselves anymore. He told me that they had a couple rough spots, but were overall very happy. They both worked fulltime, and their kids are healthy. He went on the say that they "have a safe, happy home, now, and are, overall, blessed."

He added, "Over the years I've thought about you and your family's selfless help and smiles. Life can be full of crappy people and situations, but little things like your folks' awesomeness helps me to know there are still good people out there."

I wrote back telling him that it was *Jesus* who arranged for them to be helped that day, simply because I couldn't talk from hoarseness that day, and that the only way God could get to them was to get me to shut up. We bantered and laughed, and I encouraged he and his wife to give the pastor's wife's church a chance, and go hang out there for several weeks.

It felt to good to be remembered all these years later and showed how simply acts of kindness can lead to greater hope, wholeness, and shows that Jesus won't let go of those whom for he moves mountains to reach.

If you have a passion for the broken and wounded, for the walking dead of this world, who are trapped in zombie land, and you want to know where to begin, this is your answer: *It's not necessarily in finding wisdom or in doing acts of charity. Perhaps, the best beginning of all is to simply walk your town and pray. Let Jesus take it from there.*

49. ANGEL AND THE PROPHET

We are a church community that dedicated ourselves and our square footage to something more than just our members and our worship service. Many of us spent too many years where the unintentional but underlying message of our church to the community around us was, "If you come to our turf, during our times, on our terms, then and *only* then will we help you or provide a space for you to learn and grow."

There is a richness to being a genuine hub in the community, on open terms. Lives are changed socially, spiritually, emotionally, and economically in our house. We now serve the Kingdom of God beyond our control and we serve the community around us beyond our abilities.

I hear whispers of leaders who are saying, nationally, that our models for church growth and church planting are in trouble. The generations coming behind are post-Christian and many of our basic assumptions and strategies for outreach and church growth from the past won't work in the future. Church plants are struggling, economically, more than ever. Large churches can still attract people with their gravitational pull. Small churches can no longer depend on passing the plate to pay for it all. Something new must be built.

I'm small and rather hidden in my own corner of the world, so these big discussions mostly pass me by. One leader, though, recently told me that what we've built here might end up being one of the kinds of prototypes, or models, which will need to be considered by church planting pastors in the future. I know a couple of local pastors who even started breweries and do church in there. But I do know one thing... it will take a different kind of pastor to lead such churches. You are either born one of the new breed or you allow Jesus to hammer you into one on his anvil. Of course, I got the latter method.

In January 2013, we had met the funeral-talking leaders who whispered to me in hushed tones about the sad but imminent demise of our ministry; around the same time, we were desperately clawing at longshot, lifesaving, economic strategies to stay afloat (which would be doomed to fail) just after we quietly put the building up for sale, as a cautionary act to hedge our final bets; when we did fail, I was invited to hear a prophet.

My friend Angel invited me to come to his downtown, Saturday, noon gathering to hear a guy, named Mike Danforth, speak. "He's a gifted prophet," Angel assured me. "I feel strongly you're supposed to be there." People always say that when making the invitation to hear a prophet.

I like Angel. He's a pastor who works with fringe people, the kind of people most others wouldn't associate with. He doesn't have a church, as much as he has a following. He sometimes rents our space to hold worship events at which time numerous people from various churches combine to hold a service. There's limited preaching, but there are words of encouragement, prophetic prayers, songs, flag-waving, and dancing. People have been known to fall, and stay down for a while. Not my kind of thing.

Angel met Jesus and got saved while marching in a gay pride parade in Hollywood, back in the eighties, before it was a mark of open-mindedness, fashionableness, tolerance, and liberal-coolness to march in a gay pride parade. After the parade, while standing on a street corner, sobered up from being strung-out all day, he cried out in a desperate manner that, if God was real, then to come meet him. He had an almost Apostle-Paul-Damascus-Road-like experience, and he never looked back. He wrote a book about his conversion called, *Over the Rainbow* (Angel Willson, 2017; Publisher, Dorothy's Club). (You can understand that Angel isn't your normal kind of pastor).

I don't run in Angel's circles; nor do I run with his congregational types, his theology types, his ultra-signs, wonders and prophecies. I'm a lesser signs and wonders, wise-cracking cynic, and probably have a stronger gift of sarcasm than prophecy. But we knew each other from working with street people. I went to hear his prophet friend, against my better judgement.

As the meeting began, Angel asked me to tell a little bit about our ministry to the street people.

"We feed the poor." Blah, blah, blah. "We give away coats and gloves." Blah, blah, blah. I was tired, worn out, and going through the most desperate and futile phase of ministry, at that time. I kept it light; I kept it brief; I went into very little detail about our situation or our status. Secretly, I thought we would close before the year was out. Mike spoke for about an hour. Just at the end of his sermon he turned to me, as I was standing at the back of the room, and said this, (I also have it on video):

Let me just say this if can to you brother; When you were speaking I saw something happening in territory, I saw like another facility, I saw an increase. In other words, keeping, almost keeping what you have but God expanding you and expanding you because of favor that is upon you. You have actually penetrated something – not something new but you've taken it to a different level. And you planted a seed. There was something that you did in the spirit- in God, where you made a decision to do something and it could have been for the worse, it looked like it could be for the worse, but it was actually for the greater.

I saw all of sudden something up here, another facility and then another facility. And so, I'm saying this; that God has you on the threshold of expansion, and the reason being is because there are partnerships there are people that are now aligning themselves with you. They are looking, some are still looking from afar off, but this year there are certain people that are going come and partner themselves with you and to help you do certain things. There are business people, there are people that have visions, they have, you know whatever, but they are not just in to being with the poor or doing whatever. They're actually there because their minds are education their minds are 'bringing up.' I'm saying this to say; that I see this school that is rising and as people enter into this place, and all of a sudden, the identities to rise up that were wiped out from under them you going to give them a place where they can come up into this mind and not be as great as but greater than. And there are people who are going to assist you in that and bring you into that because this part of the double portion.

I say double portion, the other part of you because you actually have a business mind in you – you have these characteristic that are inside of you and the spirit of the Lord says

'Now I'm going to take you as priest and I'm going to take you as a king – two are inside of you, the two are married; so, you are now going to be married to people who are of a like heart and like mind. And it is going to rise up in a huge way.'

The spirit of the Lord says it's because there is a humility that is inside of you. You are not out to be brilliant, out to shine, or do whatever. You really are, in your heart, you just laid it all down and said, 'Lord whatever it is that you want me to do, I'm willing to do that,' and people are beginning to see that. In other words, they are realizing that they can trust you. They have watched you for a season and watched you for a time. And you did certain things but now a trust has developed, and they realize you aren't out there just to build your own house, but you're really are out there to help people become who they are destined to be in God.

So, something huge is going to shift. And I'm not talking about property that is just like; here I'll give you this. I'm talking about primary property. I'm talking about property that only people with millions of dollars would be able to get their hands on. This is the favor of God, which is upon your life and upon your house and upon your seed. I just declare that in Jesus name.

At that point, the people began to favorably applaud and then asked him to tell the story about Ireland and he simply moved on in his story telling. I'm sure he has no memory of this day or these words. But I remember.

On the video, the camera pans over to me as he spoke the words. I'm standing there in my brown sweatshirt with my hands in the pockets leaning against a wall just staring at him with my best poker face. I recall feeling this incredible tingling and warmth has he spoke the prophetic words. The cynic in me needed the personal experiential element from God to confirm what was being said, but at the same time I was thinking to myself "School?" What the heck, I have no interest in creating a school!"

Nine months later, people with millions of dollars came along and offered to buy our church. But in the end, we kept that facility for over two more years, even as we bought a primary property of anchor tenant quality in a new neighborhood. In the same month he prophesied, as we lay dying, a few key families decided to join our church. Some of them would become top leaders helping get us through the next season. We built a job training school using our café. If we ever grow begin enough, we plan on doing it again with a Gathering House North or Gathering House South. If all he said is accurate – God already has the next place in mind.

The day Angel insisted I go to hear his prophet friend I was toying with other possible futures for my life, ones that did not include ministry. From my perspective, I was like that cup of coffee you drink while working in the garage, the one you set down somewhere and can't find, so you just go get a new cup. I felt like God's half-sipped coffee cup. I was sure He'd forgotten where He'd set me and He'd just moved on with other people. Five years on the bottom of society looking up will do that to a person.

My wife and I, our family, and a handful others endured a long season from apocalyptic fallout to living among the walking dead of street society. We dragged a church from its own zombie state to place where Jesus could heal it and give it back a new life.

The road would twist and turn many times over. Even now as I write this, three and half years from the time of the prophecy, it still feels like the adventure is just getting underway. But now it feels like the boat is sailing on the currents of life instead of just taking on water.

Jesus is an incredible pilot, but he likes to take us by way of the winds and rocks. I've decided he doesn't like straight courses. He doesn't like smooth water as much as rough waves and high winds. Jesus likes the danger and the adventure. He is a God who loves putting us in unpredictable and impossible circumstances and then rescuing us, at the last minute. He does this because we change more radically under the wildness of life and He gets more glory from grand adventures and miraculous rescues.

ABOUT THE AUTHOR

Rob Bryceson is the pastor of The Gathering House in Spokane, WA. He has a Masters in Divinity from Western Seminary, a Graduate Certificate in Ministry from Multnomah School of the Bible, and holds a Bachelor's Degree in Education from Eastern Washington University with a History Major and minors in both Government and English.

Rob has been a published songwriter, a musician, and singer. He has served on numerous boards for groups that serve the underprivileged or done overseas missions work. He is the co-founder of Street Wise, a ministry to the poor and underprivileged.

Rob and his wife Tonia have raised five wonderful children into their adult lives. They could not be prouder of them. Family Sunday night dinner around the table is still the highlight of their lives.

For booking information or speaking engagements contact:
rob@gatheringhouse.org

For additional Information see

www.streetwisespokane.org

www.gatheringhouse.org